TESTIMONIALS

The history of America is filled with contradictions. Inspiration and desperation. Patriotism and racism. Extreme wealth and poverty. What makes *Self-Elected* such an excellent book is that Lisa's story is an authentic look at one person's journey navigating those contradictions. Most importantly, her book creates the permission for leaders to celebrate the obstacles we've beaten and recognize the privileges that may have played an outsized role in overcoming them. Read *Self-Elected* if you are ready to go beyond profits and leverage your business to push for a more equitable America.

Scott Case, founding CTO of priceline.com +
Chair of Network for Good

In a time when there is a desperate need for counter-cultural thinking about profits, its purpose and its impact on people, Lisa Wise delivers a challenge to all of us in business: intentional self-lessness. *Self-Elected* is an experiential treatise on doing justice in business; it stands out as the conscientious objector of doing things the way they have always been done. It is a must-read for new entrepreneurs, those who have been at it some time, and those who may be seeking a path different from what the prevailing culture has considered true success.

Rahsaan Bernard, President, Building Bridges Across the River

Self-Elected is the perfect kind of business book for entrepreneurs to read at any stage of their journey. Part memoir, part how-to guide, Lisa's story shows us that putting people over profit can also lead to financial success. But a little warning, don't read this if you are not ready to take action—this book reminds you of your civic role as a leader to make this a more equitable and prosperous world for all.

Stacey Price, Co-Founder + Chief Localist, Shop Made in DC

Individuals who desire to venture into social impact entrepreneur-ship often struggle with the misconception that you won't make much money creating a mission-driven business. Others battle with the guilt that you shouldn't make money since zero-sum theory has paralyzed some to believe that revenue means taking away from others you serve. I hope you grant yourself the permission to read *Self-Elected* by Lisa Wise and take part in a community that believes in a positive-sum change. A belief that everyone wins when com-panies are positioned based on the core values of sharing profits, valuing employees, and serving communities. Wise reminds us that purpose means profit—for all.

Joanna Ha Yean Shin, Architecture + Human Rights, Project Manager Real Estate Development – APAH

Lisa Wise's book is an ode to purpose-driven leadership as it tracks her life journey. Her focus on profit with purpose is a model business leaders should adapt and could lead the way to a more inclusive and equitable community for us all. She is someone to watch.

Alex Orfinger, Market President + Publisher
at Washington Business Journal

If you're frustrated with the state of the world, find yourself wondering what went wrong, or feel stumped about how you can still make a meaningful difference here in the 21st century, read Lisa Wise's wonderful new book! You'll get an inside look at how she turns life lessons in landladying, Lean management, and social justice into practical lessons that she turned into a ground-breaking, purpose-driven, systems-focused, still profitable, community-based business. If you read Lisa's book you'll be able to turn her teachings into a difference-making organization of your own! Her practical, powerful, and purposeful lessons are applicable in every walk of life! If the world were led by women like Lisa Wise, this would be a far more caring, more collaborative, and more creative planet!

Ari Weinzweig, CEO of Zingerman's

Self-Elected and Lisa Wise herself are testaments to the power a business and an individual can have. Every one of us has an ability to create change if we want it badly enough and are willing to put the work into making it happen. Lisa's belief that everyone wins when we put people before profits is a model that every leader should live by. If you are ready to take the next step in upleveling your thinking and ways of being then *Self-Elected* is a must-read for you.

Jenn T. Grace, Founder, Publisher, + CEO,
Publish Your Purpose & Co-Founder +
Board Chair, B Local Connecticut

Self-Elected is unlike any business book you've read before. In these pages, successful entrepreneur and housing justice visionary Lisa Wise provides an elegant counterpoint to the notion that designing and running a competitive, profitable company is at odds with creating a more equitable world. She shows how a for-profit business can meaningfully advance justice by expanding access to wealth accumulation and housing security, and that a dogged commitment to progressive values can be compatible with achieving profits and growth. This book is a powerful resource for anyone who wants to fuse profits with purpose, and is looking for inspiration, evidence, and direct, practical advice for how to do it.

Sarah Stein Greenberg, Executive Director of the Stanford d.school (Hasso Plattner Institute of Design at Stanford University)

Self-Elected by Lisa Wise will make you smile, dream, hope, and create the world we need.

When we lead with money and not humanity, we have a world filled with oppression. Profit and equity can stand tall together, and through each word, Lisa gives us the road map to make it a reality. This book is a must-read if you are an entrepreneur, leader, politician, educator, or activist. I highly recommend *Self-Elected* for anyone desiring a more just and equitable world.

Ruby "SunShine" Taylor, Founder +
CEO of the Financial Joy School

Doing right, doing good, and doing well aren't mutually exclusive. Contrary to popular belief, it's possible to create a business that serves the community, offers employees a wonderful place to build their careers, and makes a sizable profit in the process. Lisa Wise shares an inspiring story of learning, understanding, and serving as she develops a suite of businesses that outperform the competition by leading with purpose. If you want to be inspired and encouraged to operate with greater intentionality and meaning in your business and your life, this book will show you the way.

Joey Coleman, Professional Speaker +
Writer on All Things Customer and
Employee Experience

SELF-ELECTED

SELF-ELECTED

HOW TO PUT JUSTICE OVER PROFIT AND SOAR IN BUSINESS

lisa wise

Edited By

Ericka Taylor

For permission requests, write to the publisher, addressed "Attention: Permissions Coordinator," at the address below.

Publish Your Purpose
141 Weston Street, #155
Hartford, CT, 06141

The opinions expressed by the Author are not necessarily those held by Publish Your Purpose.

Ordering Information: Quantity sales and special discounts are available on quantity purchases by corporations, associations, and others. For details, contact the publisher at orders@publishyourpurposepress.com.

Edited by: Kassandra White, Chloë Siennah
Cover design by: Cornelia Murariu
Typeset by: Medlar Publishing Solutions Pvt Ltd., India
Headshot by: Bill Gentle

Printed in the United States of America.
ISBN: 978-1-955985-62-8 (hardcover)
ISBN: 978-1-955985-61-1 (paperback)
ISBN: 978-1-955985-63-5 (ebook)

Library of Congress Control Number: 9781955985611

First edition, October 2022.

The information contained within this book is strictly for informational purposes. The material may include information, products, or services by third parties. As such, the Author and Publisher do not assume responsibility or liability for any third-party material or opinions. The publisher is not responsible for websites (or their content) that are not owned by the publisher. Readers are advised to do their own due diligence when it comes to making decisions.

Publish Your Purpose is a hybrid publisher of non-fiction books. Our authors are thought leaders, experts in their fields, and visionaries paving the way to social change—from food security to anti-racism. We give underrepresented voices power and a stage to share their stories, speak their truth, and impact their communities. Do you have a book idea you would like us to consider publishing? Please visit PublishYourPurpose.com for more information.

DEDICATION

To my grandmother, whose loving
embrace never let me turn back.
Fly high, Grandma Sue.

TABLE OF CONTENTS

Acknowledgments . . . . *xvii*

Foreword . . . . *xxi*

Prologue: Security as Justice . . . . *xxv*

PART ONE

Chapter 1: The Justice Advantage 3

Chapter 2: Getting Justice 9

Chapter 3: Landladying 15

PART TWO

Chapter 4: Framing Up the Business—Keeping it Lean 25

Chapter 5: A Problem is an Opportunity 41

Chapter 6: The Business Case for Justice and the Justice
            Case for Business 45

PART THREE

Chapter 7:   Forever Starting 55

Chapter 8:   Method to the Madness 75

PART FOUR

Chapter 9:   Different Out of the Gate 129

PART FIVE

Chapter 10: People + The Culture of Servant Leadership . . .165

Chapter 11: Purpose in Partnership. 179

Chapter 12: The Culture of Security: Don't Be Afraid
to Be Afraid. 201

PART SIX

Chapter 13: Abundance in Practice 221

Epilogue: Take Care of One Another 263

Speaking & Consulting 267

About Flock, birdSEED, BirdWatch. 269

About the Author 271

Bibliography 273

ACKNOWLEDGMENTS

Since I was a pig-tailed tomboy, I had big plans even if I lacked experience. I seemed to have infinite endurance for work, and passion in abundance. I convinced myself easily that none of my crazy ideas would be very hard to pull off. They always are, though. This book is no exception. To date, *Self-Elected* has been the most challenging project of my lifetime. I lacked the experience, the courage, and the confidence I thought it took to write a book. So, I tried shortcuts. Like any smart executive, I thought, "I can hire for that!" But no ghostwriter could tell this story. None among us shared my bumpy past and leveraged it in favor of working on a smoother future for all. So, while it may be unconventional, I'm going to congratulate myself. I found words and a voice I didn't know I had. The risk was transformational. But before I could listen to that voice, a small and fierce audience confirmed for me that I had something important to share. Without them, the story of *Self-Elected* would remain untold.

I'm grateful to my son Beckett, who would often exclaim when I shared progress on the book, "Mommio!!! That's so wonderful." He offered his own patience with my progress reports, pondering adult non-fiction cuddled up with his own elementary fiction books. He made me feel proud of the work and the words. To my Flock and BirdWatch colleagues—my work family. These companies and the leadership made room for this book and for me to find the time to write it. They spent a decade joking: "That should go in the book!!!" Little did they know. It's my pleasure and honor to be their servant leader.

The practicality of writing a book was a team sport for me. With me, every step of the way was Maureen Cain. As my book producer, she was my thought partner, cheerleader, head checker, and champion for the work. Together, during the heaviest and darkest days of the pandemic, we joined together on Zoom and hung out in shared documents as the themes, chapters, stories and the calls to action began to unfold. It wasn't lost on us that as the book became clearer, the world around us became murkier. *Self-Elected* offered each of us an outlet and an anchor at once. This partnership was rounded out by Ericka Taylor. She contributed her editorial expertise, a fierce vision of a just world, and unwavering support as the book began to take shape and later, started reading and looking like a book. She was tender with my words but helped shape and hone my storytelling.

In the last chapter, I was joined by Publish Your Purpose Press and professional superhero Jenn. T. Grace. The publishing support and expertise delivered by her team really did make this dream come true and they indulged what is likely nails on a chalkboard for any publisher—I have a preference for my name in lower case. It just feels right to be lisa wise.

To Natasha, Mark, Sharon, and Frances. You kept reading. You kept listening. It took three years for this book to find its way to a shelf. Every single day, you were the wind at my back. Thanks for introducing me to my own courage and helping me soar.

And to my wife, Cameron. Who heard all these stories again, with an open heart and a curiosity I'm deeply grateful for. I'll keep taking chances.

FOREWORD

I believe that each and every one of us has the power to impact change in ways both big and small. Systemic issues feel big—and they are—but systems are created by people, after all. Therefore, it is imperative that people, both individually and collectively, take steps to change the systems that are not working.

As a journalist, I look to uncover the stories of people who are agents of positive change, those on the ground challenging the status quo and building new pathways forward that serve the greater good. I first spoke to Lisa Wise when I interviewed her for a *Forbes* article titled "People Over Profit: How One Founder Is Combating Housing Inequality," and was struck by how Lisa is running an ethical, intentional company and turning a profit that benefits both herself and her employees. At the same time, her company is also making her community a better place.

I'd been reporting on how more equitable public policies and financial regulations are essential for leveling inequities, but lisa is an example of a business leader taking it upon herself to do her part in creating a more equitable society where she can—in this case, the housing market.

To me, the spirit of "self elected" is about not waiting for things to change, but stepping into your own power to make change happen when and where you can. It's also about inspiring others to come along with you, because there is strength in numbers and community matters.

This essential paradigm shift is key for the sustainability of ourselves, our country, and our planet. *Self Elected* is a rallying cry to leave the binary thinking of win-lose behind, where companies place profit above all else and are built on the backs of their workers. In this paradigm, only the leaders or key stakeholders reap the benefits. A sustainable future requires justice-based business where employees, communities and the environment also benefit.

In *Self Elected*, Lisa shares her honest journey to creating a just business with a mindset that focuses on what is *possible* rather than what *is*. It's about moving from a scarcity mindset to an abundance mindset. It's about creating companies that are win-win.

This book is a reminder that we are the ones we've been waiting for. It's tapping into the larger cultural transformation that I believe is already under way. From employees taking back their power and quitting in record numbers in what has been dubbed The Great Resignation when they aren't getting the conditions they need, to the wave of employee-led activism sparking union wins at Fortune 500 companies such as Amazon and Starbucks, individuals are self electing to take matters into their own hands.

The most successful businesses will understand that when their employees are thriving, so too does their company. Lisa's Flock is a shining example of how taking care of your team first is the fuel that gives companies the ability to also take care of their company and their community. It's time to change how businesses measure profit. If a company makes a billion dollars while burning out their workers and pillaging the environment, is that really a valuable return? The cost to human capital, the community and environment should also be integral to metrics of success. This is not to say that money does not matter, but making money the only goal has destructive costs that far outweigh the advantage to the bottom line. The story of Flock is a guidepost for how purpose leads to profit when you put people and place above it.

Lisa does this by focusing on home, the place where we build a life, make memories, connect with loved ones and find solace. Homeownership has been a traditional path to building intergenerational wealth. Owning a home allows you to build equity, make a profit if you decide to sell, or pass on assets to family members in an inheritance.

Yet inequities have existed for decades that make the path to home ownership more challenging for people of color. For example, the research shows that Black people are more likely to be denied credit, especially for mortgages, and receive worse rates when they are approved. Public policies such as redlining, which essentially sanctioned segregation when the government mapped out "safe" areas to insure mortgages that excluded African American communities, contributed to the persistent racial wealth gap. We're seeing this play out in ongoing housing inequality: In the fourth quarter of 2021,

74% of White adults owned a home, compared with 43% of Black Americans and 48% of Hispanic Americans, according to the Pew Research Center.

Self-Elected is both the story of how our past does not need to dictate our future, and how individuals and businesses can have a real impact on changing the course of systemic inequities from becoming further entrenched. It's also a story about coming home to ourselves, sparking us to identify our personal purpose and ways we can make an impact.

No promises that the journey will be easy, but it is worth embarking upon. The enduring bottom line is this: May you know your power. May you see the possibilities. May you step forward to become self elected.

Holly Corbett, *Forbes* contributor &
VP of Content, Consciously Unbiased

PROLOGUE:
SECURITY AS JUSTICE

I met my best friend, Myrtle Friedman, on a tree-lined street in small-town Idaho in the late 1970s. Myrtle was 80(ish) years my senior and lived alone, next door to our small family of four. Her two-story, green stucco house was perched on the corner, just two blocks from Main Street. On a special Saturday, here and there, my family would arrange to let Myrtle back her vintage Cadillac out of the single car garage and take it around the block with our dog, Sam, tucked in her lap. I took the backseat. It seemed reasonably safe. For eight-year-old me, reasonably safe was a big win. I always looked forward to those drives. It felt like a village coming together to honor freedom, even if that freedom unfolded on a single square block, unbothered with signage or sidewalks for that matter.

During all the in-between days, I would tend to Myrtle's rhubarb, weed her vegetable garden, and listen to her tell stories in a stuffy living room that looked exactly like you might imagine it—dusty, patterned, and threadbare—but to my fresh eyes, it was grand as could be. For my chores, I got paid in hard candy, which I enjoyed as she told me about her life and shared her memories. Good and bad. Myrtle had lived through both World Wars and the Great Depression. In that room, I felt protected from the insecurity and chaos of my own house. Myrtle's simple care and concern, her willingness to engage and connect with me not only eased my loneliness, it soothed my anxiety about the looming Cold War and all other uncertainties in my life that left me in a constant state of unease and worry. After all, if Myrtle had found her way to the other side of 80, surely there was a bit of freedom for me to look forward to in life.

Myrtle offered balance during that rocky time. She offered an emotional shelter and a familiar and safe space. At least before we were on the move again. I had lived in 23 different spaces over six states in 12 different towns and mid-sized cities by the time I went to college in 1990. My earliest years were spent bouncing from one public school to another across Southern Idaho. Each one kept stunningly low standards for education, and moving so often meant I was a child left behind. It's a miracle I (eventually) learned to read, let alone wrote a book. Thanks to this rocky start, I developed a strong sense of justice and determined early on that nobody should suffer insecurity. I wanted everyone to have a safe home of their own. I wanted to build a life that could shelter others from adversity, even if I didn't know them, while at the same time maximizing safety and security for myself and those closest to me. I wanted to advance social justice. So I elected myself to do just that.

Ever since choosing that path for my life, my journey has been rich, and my impact has, too. Today, I have security in abundance, both personally and professionally. My nuclear family enjoys financial stability and—a personal dream—calls a safe and lovely house our home. With an eye toward helping others achieve the same, I started Flock, a family of real estate management companies that tends to well over two billion dollars in property in Washington, DC. We care for dignified and safe homes along with the residents who live in them. We embrace and contribute to our community as an act of justice. We put people and place over profit, and we soar.

When I made the scary transition from employee to employer in 2008, I knew this social justice lens would light the path to traditional profitability. If I led with purpose and values, the money would follow. I posit here, everyone profits with a socially just business paradigm. I built a family of companies that aren't just profitable in terms of net income but are also rich in community impact. Here, I will share the strategies and stories about how Flock took flight. I explain how, in just over a decade, we've captured exceptional market share. How we're in the top 10% of average industry earnings. How we enjoy local and national media exposure for our work, including features in the *Washington Post*, *The Hill*, and business fan favorites that include *Fast Company*, *Forbes*, and many more. How we have a metaphorical trophy cabinet with proud placements in various "best place to work" and "best of" contests. How we've emerged as a top regional philanthropist in the *Washington Business Journal* year after year and enjoyed ranking among Inc. 5000's fastest growing companies regionally and nationally. How we're called upon as industry and issue experts, consulting on local, regional, and federal housing policy and law. And these are mere highlights.

We are not outliers. Since 1985, Patagonia has given over $140 million to grassroots environmental groups working to protect the natural environment. They have a deep understanding of the ties between social justice and saving the environment. Yvon Chouinard, their founder, has said, "This is not philanthropy. This should be a cost of doing business. It's paying rent for our use of the planet."[1]

Like Flock, Patagonia operates as a justice-based company. Justice-based companies create good jobs with benefits and wraparound support for the employee as a person, not just an asset. Just businesses support and fight for policies and laws that protect the underserved, support the marginalized, and pursue equality. Justice-based businesses fight racism. Just businesses prioritize corporate philanthropy, public advocacy, and volunteering. Sharing the abundance of resources and giving visibility and exposure to causes is second nature to a just business. And social justice companies can also be deeply profitable. Decade over decade, Patagonia performs as one of the most highly-respected and highly-rated outdoor clothing makers in the industry. Patagonia puts people and the

---

[1] 1% For the Planet, "Home Page."

planet first—and it is valued at over a billion dollars, leaving plenty to invest in people and the planet.

So, how did we design and operationalize a social justice business in an often unethical and almost always disliked industry? It's what this book is all about. I explain how I built and still run a company that puts stakeholders first. I tell you how to be profitable while being an agent of change. I offer tactical and practical strategies for running a purpose-driven, social justice company. I also feature other companies, like Patagonia, that prove investing in justice for people and places is a win-win. And I explain why, simply put, it's the only kind of business to be in. You and society soar in this world view.

Throughout this book, I leverage the story of my journey to provide insights and justifications for justice-based business because I believe the pathway to justice and profits doesn't need to be complicated. The first half illustrates what it takes to make this model work. It offers practical guidance on how to design and operate your business with a justice lens and profit. I illustrate how we used the **lean startup framework** to continuously inform our business model and drive our operational design. I detail how Flock and other companies **differentiate** themselves, build fans for life, and stand out because they are standing up. Finally, I express why and how the **servant leadership** model is the best investment you can make in your company, your team, and your community. I also spotlight some of our failures and false starts—because trial and error replaced the business education I never got.

The second half of the book makes the societal, political, cultural, and environmental case for social-justice-based businesses. Not only does this model have a competitive advantage, it's an investment in solving problems that threaten our future, our country, our community, our neighbors, our kids. Us. We need this investment. We can elect to pursue a bright and prosperous future for *all* while fighting climate change, racism, inequity, poverty, and health disparities globally. Because the future is at risk when the prize in business is profit alone.

Note to the reader: This book is a series of stories, theories, disruptive concepts, and profiles of individuals and companies that are getting it right. It contains plenty of how-to content and replicable strategies that will give you the justice advantage we've leveraged with great success. However, this isn't a workbook or a step-by-step guide or, technically, even a business book. What we did and what we're advocating for is a business model that maps a path to contributing to the collective good with the added advantage of profitability because we believe companies and the economy can and should create room for all to fly high.

PART ONE

CHAPTER 1

THE JUSTICE ADVANTAGE

Having a business that advances justice isn't just supporting causes, policies, and practices that are better for the community, the environment, and society. Justice needs to be reflected in the company design, operations, and leadership. When justice is at play internally and externally, the work is more meaningful, and financial profit is inevitable. Social justice values differentiate companies, attract buyers and clients, and build fans for life. Those values start at the "home office." We can't make the world a more just place unless we make life better and more abundant for our team, which means leading with justice.

That's why we share 40% of profits with our staff. Every single year. We don't consider our benefits plan to be a cost as much as an essential investment in the people who carry out the work. Our corporate embrace includes three months of fully paid family leave. We underwrite continuing education, 401k matches, and 529 contributions and offer student loan payment support. Company ownership opportunities are extended to every team member, and long- and short-term disability and health care are 100% covered.

Americans have a strong history of individual giving in their communities: Our levels of volunteerism and philanthropy are higher in the United States than in any other country. More and more companies should openly embrace the value of volunteering and offer benefits like company-wide volunteer days, volunteer time off, or giving programs matched by the company. Our companies create space for and endorse good citizenship. We support and honor team members' participation in volunteer programs, as well as their board roles.

No less significantly, we support team members in advancing their careers. In fact, Flock is designed to give team members mobility (lateral or upward) without leaving the company. We did this because we wanted to create career homes. According to Willis Towers Watson, over 70% of "high-retention-risk" employees want to leave because they see no future advancement in the current job,[2] and a study by Hays Recruiting found that 71% of employees would accept a pay cut, just to get a better job.[3] This shows just how wrong businesses are when they assume employees leave for more

---

[2]Willis Towers Watson, "2021 Talent Attraction and Retention Survey."

[3]HAYS US, "US Workers Willing to Compromise on Salary for the Right Benefits, Company Culture, and Career Growth Opportunities."

money. Better pay is only an issue for 12% of people who leave a company, according to a survey by Career Builder.[4]

We reimagine profit, factoring in the number of good jobs we create, the quality of benefits, the financial and time commitments we make to our community, and the support and nurturing of talent, in addition to keeping our books in the black. All of this differentiates us. And different is our normal.

Fortunately for us, consumers want companies that do things differently and lead with their values. They aren't just buying products or services; they are also building on a relationship with a company with which they are choosing to do business. I'm putting an emphasis on choice. Certainly, food and shelter choices may hinge more on price or accessibility, but even the most basic consumer purchase typically comes with an astonishing number of choices. Think about how many toothpaste brands, meal kits, or dog walkers you might choose from. In DC, there are so many real estate agents that they might as well be the state bird. In a hyper-competitive business landscape, whether you operate a service, technical, or product-driven company, it's hard to stand out. So I'm arguing: *Stand out by standing up for social justice.* The consumer will be there to greet you if your business helps improve their lives.

In her *Forbes* article, "How Companies Are Helping to Close The Racial Wealth Gap," Holly Corbett writes about a new antiracist business mandate: "The bottom line is that

---

[4]Career Builder, "CareerBuilder Survey Reveals a More Flexible Future Workforce."

businesses don't have to wait for public policy to help close the racial wealth gap. Indeed, customers may be looking to business to help lead the change: About 86% of consumers believe that companies should take a stand for social issues."[5] At Flock, we are meeting this moment. Later in the book, you'll learn how our signature birdSEED program was developed to fund down-payment grants to first-time BIPOC home buyers. Where there are justice gaps, we've been eager to build bridges. Importantly, this work isn't a detour for us: It is deeply emblematic of our core values. We're giving back and advancing social justice because we designed our companies to do just that.

Businesses that lead with purpose outperform their competitors. Think Warby Parker, Toms Shoes, Impossible Foods, Penzeys Spices, Farmgirl Flowers, and my brand crush, Patagonia. Living in those Idaho mountain towns, cold weather clothing was tied to personal brand, and Patagonia became the "go-to-gear" for those who could afford it. Sometime in the mid-80s, around the 5th grade, I had a single blue pilly Patagonia fleece. I think my mom had to peel it off of me in my sleep to wash. Decades later, I would learn that the same company was leading other businesses to help ensure the planet and future generations thrive through 1% for the Planet, the international nonprofit Yvon Chouinard started in 2002. With a mission of encouraging businesses to give at least 1% of their sales to help solve the climate crisis, 1% for

---

[5]Corbett, "How Companies Are Helping to Close the Racial Wealth Gap."

the Planet has given almost $300 million to nonprofit organizations around the world.

All the while, Patagonia and similarly justice-oriented businesses have shown they can generate a profit while becoming well-known for creating high-paying, high-quality-of-life jobs, leaving lighter environmental footprints, and operating under a give-back model that generates resources for the underserved. These companies can be making things as simple as shoes and glasses, and they are often found squarely within industries that were long overdue for a makeover. The products look so good and perform so well because the companies are doing things so differently from the competition—internally *and* externally.

This model works whether you are designing something new or relaunching something tired and old. It doesn't matter if you have a service-based business or if you're inventing and selling a product. The three principles we work with—a start-up framework, differentiation, and servant leadership—provide a framework for us to create a highly successful, justice-driven company that serves all stakeholders, the owner included.

Creating and operating a justice-driven business is, in some ways, a hedge. Millennials and Generation Z can no longer expect to outperform their parents, so business as usual holds less appeal for them. *Forbes* recently reported on a Gallup Poll that showed 60% of Millennials would consider leaving their jobs if they didn't feel engaged in the workplace.[6]

---

[6]McGrady, "New Survey: Three Main Reasons Why Millennials Quit Their Jobs."

As we saw above, consumers intend to spend with their values, so a business will be better positioned for success and broad client/customer appeal when it's anchored in justice. It's a key differentiator, and, even better, this type of company ethos is evergreen. Business as a pure generator of shareholder profit will die on the vine unless it learns to adapt and catches up quickly.

To truly become impactful, the business community has to go well beyond traditional corporate social responsibility goals and objectives, which are effectively checklist practices, ancillary to most businesses objectives. So, if you can improve or produce a product, service, or system while doing good in the world, I say start today. Elect yourself to advance real social change. Build and operate a company whose very fabric is designed with purpose. I guarantee the profits will come. Indeed, they did for me.

CHAPTER 2

GETTING JUSTICE

So, how did I get from the potato state to the nation's capital, running a seven-million-dollar (and growing) family of companies? The seed was planted early. At some point in elementary school, it began to dawn on me that my family lacked resources. Perhaps, it was the truck we depended on to cut and haul wood all summer, so we could stay warm in harsh Hailey, Idaho winters. That truck was three shades of green (cheap body work), and it lacked the ability to reverse. Fortunately, pulling and hauling was never a problem, and small-town Idaho delivered on space.

The instability of my childhood began long before we got to Hailey. Part of this was just being a child of the 80s, when the economy was tanking and jobs were scarce. Part of it was growing up in predominantly rural communities where small-town economies couldn't support much beyond the service industry. My PhD stepfather swung hammers on custom homes in subzero temperatures to make ends meet. My mom worked at a debt collection office. Even my biological father, who was a medical doctor, declared bankruptcy and experienced financial difficulties that created all kinds of stress for my family.

My bet is that some of us who grew up in homes where basic needs weren't always met became adults who sought out what we lacked as children. Stanford professor Steve Blank has gone a step further and theorized that the chaos so common to less-than-optimally-functional families creates adults who are exceptionally well-positioned to become successful entrepreneurs. He argues that having to deal with poverty or parental alcoholism or abuse or any number of unfortunate upbringings provides those of us who survive with the grit and resilience necessary to start a new business.[7] And wow, did I have grit.

As someone who grew up without a lot of stability, security was what I coveted most. And I knew that security often looked a lot like cash. Luckily enough, I was a born entrepreneur drawn to business from a very early age. I learned how to stuff a piggy bank, and I had every kind of childhood paying job you could think of—and some you'd probably never imagine.

We'd landed in Hailey, Idaho, because my stepfather got a job at the Historical Society. We were there five years, the longest I would live anywhere until college. When we first

---

[7] Blank, "Why the Lean Startup Changes Everything."

arrived, we lived in a two-story house with a big concrete basement. My brother and I each had rooms on the top floor, and I would seek entertainment and shelter from the cold in the basement with a pogo stick. I tried, unsuccessfully, to find my way into the *Guinness Book of World Records* for my talents, but that goal was easy to leave behind when I realized there was no cash prize for record breaking.

I loved that house, but I recognized in a deep way that it wasn't ours. It was a rental. I remember my parents' anxiety about living in that house, and I didn't like knowing we had to get permission for something as simple as hanging a picture. Life was already too complicated for my elementary school self, and I struggled to enjoy anything that felt temporary or impermanent. I wanted the security of ownership. This need probably explains how I became a child motivated, not by dreams of babies and weddings, but by a desire to be a leader in business and to keep others from experiencing what was so painful for me. I wanted justice.

Conveniently, for a budding businesswoman, Hailey, Idaho—population roughly 1,800—was my oyster. The upside of being the youngest with thin support from my working parents was my freedom. I was getting myself to and from the fourth grade on foot, bicycle, or even cross country skis if the road conditions called for it. I could do what I wanted. That freedom of movement meant there were an abundance of business opportunities. While Hailey wasn't the biggest market in the world, I worked it hard. I'd heard somewhere that persistence is everything in sales, so I knocked on every single door in town, over and over again. It turned out that earning cash was easy. I saw dollar signs everywhere I looked. To finance summer camp, I sold around two thousand boxes of Girl Scout cookies in a town of eighteen hundred people—a population-to-sales success ratio I haven't been able to replicate since. Plus, all that door-knocking was great for building my vacuum-cleaning, car-washing, pet-sitting, and sidewalk-shoveling business development pipeline.

Hailey, adjacent to famous Sun Valley, is a ski town. Demi Moore, Dianna Ross, Clint Eastwood, and many other Hollywood elites sometimes resided in that valley or visited regularly. Being on the downside of the haves and have-nots meant that I was turned off by excess even at that young age. There wasn't anything I admired about the haves, though I did covet their stable housing, mobility, and killer ski pants. Instead, I found the idea of people having far more than they actually needed to be particularly off putting. It wasn't like I saw people with resources being more caring or charitable or warmly embracing those with less. In fact, the frivolous nature of that wealth made me embrace the values of our struggling household over those of our wealthy neighbors. That's because we needed and offered help. We shared bounty from the garden, worked on each other's houses, and had meals together often. We shoveled sidewalks for the infirm, checked on each other's houses, and watched out for each other's kids. Even when there was scarcity, we still had an abundance mindset.

Don't get me wrong. I wasn't satisfied with an abundance mindset if it really just meant we shared green beans with the neighbors. I wanted real wealth and financial security for myself and others. The difference between the snow bunny set and my big plan was my desire to give back, to redistribute wealth, to smooth out inequity, and to create opportunity not just for me but for society. I wanted justice. And in advancing justice, what did I have to lose?

Scarcity-based business models offer substantial context for how companies are designed to hoard profits and hesitate to invest in their teams, their community, and the environment. Scarcity is antithetical to justice. I believe, in business and in life, there is plenty to go around. Flock, our family of companies, intentionally built a culture of abundance, and that allows for breathing room. It offers more security and hope. It inspires teamwork and collaboration. A scarcity-based business model compels competition, aggression, and tension. Yet it seems to be the favored approach in capitalism. It's Darwinian in nature, but laws of nature should be tested.

I chose a different path. I chose to profit share, to give most of the fruits of the labor to those who actually did the labor. In this, I'm not aligned with my business peers. If they were to study the "sacrifices" I've made, some might argue I gave away the farm. Over the last decade or so, I've provided my team with bonuses and benefits that equate to roughly a million dollars and that wouldn't be considered "necessary" components of a fair compensation model. When you pair these dollars with the investments we made in the company's growth, it's clear that for a business our size, it was not an insignificant amount. Those dollars in almost every other company setting, especially in the property management industry, would have lined the pockets of the owner. I could be enjoying a nicer house or more extravagant vacations or fancier cars. I could be accumulating wealth to pass on to future generations and structuring my legacy based on bloodlines and family ties. But I don't want my abundance to depend on scarcity for others. While the math is harder to perform, I believe I'm much wealthier today precisely because I distribute the fruits of *our* labor. My legacy can be measured in the loyalty my business model has inspired. Our average tenure is four years, with our first hire still calling Flock her work home. Turnover plagues the industry at over 36%,[8] but the loyalty and the engaged enthusiasm from the vast majority of my team members (not to mention clients), I believe, has led to greater success and profitability.

Abundance, a sharing-based business model, is more sophisticated. It is deeply just, and while it may be a long game, I believe it's the game with the fairest rules and the greatest probability of a big win. And in the world of housing management, we need more wins and more abundance.

---

[8] Home365, "Employee Retention in Property Management."

CHAPTER 3

LANDLADYING

Though managing home was a natural destination for me, how I found myself there is a tender story. When I settled into college life in Tucson, Arizona, far from my fractured family, I got a call from my Aunt Susan letting me know that, surprisingly, I had a first cousin once removed who lived in the area. I took down his number and after hanging up the phone, imagined myself enjoying a home cooked meal with Richard and his wife. Certainly, they lived somewhere tucked in the popular foothills far from my low-cost student housing. I was eager to be in touch but also curious why I had never heard about Richard. It's true our family wasn't tight-knit, but I didn't recall us leaving family members out of conversation.

I arranged to meet Richard at a residential intersection in Barrio Santa Rosa—a historic neighborhood with a mix of shotgun railroad adobes and lots of one-room guest houses. One of which, it turned out, Richard called home. We planned for coffee and dessert at the popular Hotel Congress, an iconic destination downtown for locals, complete with (actual) penny tile floors and a salty staff. When I first spotted Richard, it was immediately clear there wouldn't be any home-cooked meal prepared by his wife. Richard was resplendent in a tight fitting pair of black jeans and his signature black leather jacket. I liked him instantly. The feeling was mutual. We were fast friends, and he oriented me to desert living, queer culture, and the world of design. He was an architect by trade, working on projects that took him around the world and designing natural habitats for zoos, piers, and, his favorite, the Siegfried and Roy cat habitat at the Mirage in Las Vegas.

Queer life in the 90s couldn't be divorced from the AIDS epidemic and the perpetual threat of HIV exposure for gay men in particular. Richard was largely estranged from his (our) family due to his "lifestyle choices," and he lived his life largely unattached to people or places that tied him down. He seemed almost cavalier about his roots or building a future. I was naive in not picking up on the story his circumstances told, but Richard was extraordinarily private about aspects of his personal life, his HIV status in particular.

Richard couldn't outrun AIDS, though he tried. He fully embraced life, art, and nature, his hedge against death. On a predictably hot summer day, Richard stopped by with a set of pencils from a Barbara Kruger collection. Each one had a saying, like "Thinking of you." He wasn't one to offer gifts, and this particular gesture was notable. Kruger, an artist famous for her bold, contemporary feminist art, said, "I'm fascinated with the difference between supposedly private and supposedly public, and I try to engage the issue of what it means to live in a society that's seemingly shock-proof, yet still is compelled to exercise secrecy."[9] That day, when I studied the lesions on Richard's face, a hallmark sign of AIDS onset, I knew the virus had caught up with him. And I knew it wasn't something he wanted to talk about. Barbara was his proxy. I still have those pencils. I don't have Richard.

Despite his protests, Richard let me care for him for several years as he suffered through AIDS. That gift of two-years of conversations was the richest and the most rewarding of my life. It created a bond not available in any other circumstances. Together, we navigated a world that blamed the victim, including a healthcare system that left gay men behind. I struggled to get Richard into trials for treatments that held little hope. Between trips to the emergency room, I tried to get support for the expensive cocktail of drugs we hoped would extend his life at thousands per month. I navigated the awkward conversations with his siblings who wanted to stay far away, and I was ashamed of them for being clearly ashamed of him. As I ran errands, folded laundry, cared for his lily pad pond, and prepped food, I pondered the injustice of it all. Both of us, largely left behind by family but tethered to each other, were kindred spirits because he was pissed off by the injustice of it all, too.

---

[9] Public Delivery, "Barbara Kruger—Your Body Is a Battleground."

He hadn't done much to prepare for the end, but during his last days in the hospital, he finally shared his game plan. First, he explained, he wanted me to leave him in the desert to naturally reunite with the landscape. I feel confident he knew that was not going to happen. He also wanted me to take his adorable, black 1993 Honda Civic. And finally, his dying wish was that I move into the house he was renting. I had spent so much time in his house, it seemed only natural that it should be mine. But as I let go of someone who anchored me, who gave me a sense of purpose and unconditional love, I wasn't interested in more uncertainty. I wanted and desperately needed a home of my own. I elected to let the lease on his rental house expire and pursue a home I could own.

When Richard died, I gathered his friends to clear the house. Each was invited to take what they pleased, the expensive drugs included. I took stock of what was left: a handful of sentimental items and the Civic, which I promptly sold for $8,300.

Then I called my (last) landlord.

In 1992 I was renting half of a sweet little 1893 adobe duplex on Rubio Avenue. White with blue framed windows and golf green doors, the house was dreamy to me, and I wanted it to be mine. The owner had moved to Australia, and I highlighted the impracticality of managing a home from half-way around the world. He agreed, and we settled on a price of $83,000—just what I needed for a 10% down payment. It was the best decision I ever made against someone's wishes. That purchase changed the entire trajectory of my life and livelihood for the better. It was a windfall I would never take for granted.

The duplex had the adobe bones I loved, but the interior featured a bare bones 80s renovation that wasn't going to work for me. I had big plans for that house, and despite a limited skillset, I wanted to move walls, build patios, fix the roof, rewire, change lights, put in new windows, plant trees, tile, and paint—to start with. But my first priority was addressing the rental, which was in rough shape but would be my money maker. The unit suffered from years of neglect: a termite-rotted subfloor that had never been completed, falling cabinets, leaking windows, and a toilet that was cracked. My tenant arranged to leave town for two weeks, so I could refresh the space. With a motley crew of friends all making their way through the quiet but oppressive heat of the Arizona summers, we buffed that unit out in no time. I was lucky and grateful for the assistance, and I paid folks in beer and pizza. When my tenant returned, I felt like an HGTV host, waiting to meet Paul at the front door and "reveal" a transformed space. I took immeasurable pride in handing over keys to an exceptional space, rather than the crap he'd left behind for two weeks. With a broad smile and big thank you, he stayed for many more years, an easy, happy tenant who I enjoyed sharing a glass of wine with in the backyard often. I loved everything about the arrangement. And I wanted more.

I would sit often in the backyard, which had piles of bricks I had scavenged from the alleyways standing by to become a patio one day. I admired the veritable grove of mesquite and palo verde saplings, which promised shade in a decade or two. This house offered endless opportunities, and the energy I got from bringing that old house to life was a driving force. I knew with great certainty I was on a path to building security for myself and others by offering quality housing. I loved working with my hands, and I wasn't sure how, but I knew I would paint many square miles worth of walls in my lifetime.

The rush of building confidence in all things building-related became a key focus as I started cultivating my physical and practical understanding of housing and construction. My go-to during those years was my good friend, Mike A. Early in my days at the University of Arizona, I crossed paths with Mike at a Pan Left Productions meeting. I started Pan Left, a video production collective, with my friend Jeff in 1992 when we set out to produce a feature-length documentary about Cuba and the Miami Cuban exile community. Naturally, one film wasn't enough, so we launched Pan Left, so we could raise tax deductible money, buy equipment, and share it with a group of political storytellers when video- and media-making tools were scarce and expensive. We rented a dusty downtown studio space for our work where we plotted and planned the stories we had to tell. One day, we were joined by someone a few years older and a lot more put together. He was wearing beige corduroy slacks and had a dress shirt that was tucked in. He seemed, at first glance, to have nothing in common with us, but Pan Left was just where he belonged. As a media specialist at the University of Arizona and someone deeply committed to social justice, Mike embodied the perfect combination of activist and realist. He had a salaried job with full benefits and spent his free time advocating for and working on causes he knew made a difference. We became fast friends.

Mike quickly understood my interest in security and stability. He too was on a journey to protect himself from uncertainty and had incredible skill in construction and home repair. He patiently, generously, and enthusiastically helped me understand the elements of a house and the nuances of the corresponding trades. He schooled me on when to call in a professional, rather than risk a DIY approach. Together, we transformed rooms. Even better, Mike helped transform my confidence. What I could do with my hands became one of the most valuable traits in my toolbox. That summer, in what were really the early days of Flock, my competitive advantage was the shared abundance mindset my community had. Just like those formative years in Idaho when we relied on neighbors to bridge caps, my Arizona community, with Mike in the lead, came through with the gift of their talent and time. That was something I would never forget. Home, financial security, abundance, and justice had found a way to merge for me because I wasn't only supporting myself—I was also finding a way to care for others.

Just like that, being a landlady became my thing. Another house here, another there, and I found myself, over the years, with a small but mighty portfolio of rentals. It was a side hustle I found not only rewarding, but impactful. I preserved historic homes, and I offered stylish, nicely-situated spaces infused with my tender loving care. Then, I rented them to folks at a little under market value, with a lot of "What can I do for you, ma'am?" service while residents enjoyed safe, secure, and dignified housing. It was a very simple formula, and it seemed almost criminal that, in the course of this arrangement, I collected rent as someone else satisfied my loan commitments. All the while, I passively enjoyed the appreciation and tax breaks to which my assets entitled me.

This ultimately proved the hypothesis I was testing all along: I could build wealth and security through housing and deliver justice with only moderate, measured risk.

I'm an experiential learner and proud of that fact. My global view of business and business practices mostly originated through trendy magazines and learn-as-you-go practices that I've since been able to organize into actual strategies that draw from business experts. I wouldn't trade this approach, and today, I'm proud to author content for some of the very same sources that helped me succeed despite my lack of industry-specific education and training.

I'm no stranger to formal, higher education, and in another, less hurried life, I might have found my way to business school at some point. But I knew starting over would come with exceptional opportunity costs. And, frankly, the required coursework didn't line up with my testing skills or academic aptitudes. It would have been painful (read: time-consuming and expensive) to get an MBA. Instead, I learned by doing, and I supplemented that by studying and learning about companies I could relate to or do business with. I read books and business magazines and listened to business podcasts, and I discovered I learned the most when I could interact with the businesses and industries I was studying or reading about.

Later, I share more stories of justice-driven or -adjacent companies. Together with my own, these examples illustrate, in very simple terms, how we've advanced justice by leveraging differentiation, servant leadership, and a startup ethos. Simply put, justice-driven business doesn't create barriers but rich opportunities for all stakeholders.

PART TWO

CHAPTER 4

FRAMING UP THE BUSINESS—KEEPING IT LEAN

A s an enthusiastic side hustler, most of my childhood jobs were squarely in the service delivery category. Laborer would also be a good word for it. Think dog walking, snow shoveling, plant watering, and the like. I got paid in cash, and scheduling happened on the home phone, provided there was someone home to take the call. None of it required a desk, but as a kid, a desk is what I really wanted—preferably one in a dedicated office where I could file lots of paperwork, stack business cards, and organize supplies.

As I grew older, I considered, in earnest, how one might manage logistics for a small and growing business. I was

fascinated with marketing, office management, communications, and budgets. I was interested in management
approaches, wondered what storefront signage might cost,
and imagined the ideal company culture and what my signature leadership style might be. I wondered where and with
whom I could make a difference. Even when I began as a
landlady, it was a side hustle. I needed something steady to
pay bills when it came time to fly as an adult. I wasn't brave
enough or prepared enough to pursue business. In fact, given
my value system and commitment to community, pursuing
wealth for the sake of it was something to be frowned upon,
by me most of all.

I studied policy and film because I loved politics, art,
and telling stories. So when it was time to focus on a career,
the nonprofit world where I could make a living advancing
important causes was a natural fit. But I was still driven by an
intense need to keep stuffing that piggy bank and kept plenty
of side hustles in play while working full time in policy and
healthcare. That cash was to hedge against unemployment,
unexpected crises, or the lack of insurance. Moonlighting was
how I found my way to landladying and, later, building, leading, and owning a real estate management company anchored
in social justice.

Yet property management and the real estate industry
are largely successful in spite of justice, not because of it.
From racist redlining to predatory lending and substandard,
poorly-serviced housing for those with less, the industry isn't
aligned with my values in the least. That's good news because

therein lies Flock's competitive advantage. Justice was, and is, our economic engine.

Today, I'm the business woman I visualized, and I'm focused on delivering a stellar work experience and inspiring excellence through a **servant leadership model**. I keep the companies in a constant state of **startup motion** with new business units, partnerships, and dynamic community initiatives. I go left if most go right, knowing that **differentiating** ourselves is a path to profitability and justice.

Despite my youthful dreams, I had no detailed plans for building a stylish, structurally-sound, well-positioned, thriving business. That lack of training led to a "learn-as-you-go," "pay-as-you-go" path that I'm proud of to this day. We framed our business, largely without a blueprint, but that's not a bad thing. In fact, we had a lean startup approach to the work, which continues to this day. As a lean startup, which I'll discuss in great detail shortly, we didn't have the resources, time, or know-how to build a company that could scale or plan for the long term. We had the time and talent to meet with potential clients, present our unique management model, and improve our service delivery as we learned, rather than anticipated, lessons along the way.

Flock took flight as a justice-based company because our lean startup ethos, servant leadership, and differentiation strategies dovetailed perfectly with our justice-based mission to amplify our success, cash profits included. I discovered how just, replicable, and responsible this strategy was compared to a more traditional, profits-first approach to capitalism.

This was the win-win model I teased out at the start of the book. We had solved a market based problem, which helped make the business case for property management, even without a business background and in an incredibly ill-regarded and complex industry, because we had infused our work with justice.

My hypothesis was simple: I theorized property management could deliver a just service—offering safe, dignified housing while creating jobs and profits and serving a community of stakeholders—at scale. From where I sat, the industry was doing none of the above. That gave me a substantial, industry-sized problem to stare down and, by extension, almost infinite opportunities to create a thriving company as one solution to that problem. While my sample size of a handful of properties in and around Tucson, Arizona, was small, it gave me real-time information about the demand for a new approach to management. And with that test under my belt, I understood the potential was substantial and there were customers ready to be served.

Unfortunately, I wasn't ready to serve them myself in the late 90s and early 2000s. Instead, I relentlessly shopped my idea to friends/acquaintances or even airline seatmates. "You should start a property management company," I would say. "It's such a great way to make a difference and make money," I offered. "Think about the passive income! It's easy to be the best by delivering the best experience." To my knowledge, nobody took me up on the idea. These were the days when I was chained to my nonprofit work because, simply put, I needed a steady paycheck. Pursuing my own "sure thing" didn't seem viable, and the timing never seemed good. I also knew it took more than a party of one to attract a client base.

As my history suggests, in business I have always wanted to stand out and stand up at the same time. But standing up alone isn't always possible (or fun), and it can be hard to get out of the starting gate alone. That's what kept me from pursuing my self-described "sure thing." I needed to do a better sales job—on myself. I also needed someone who could share, or at least make a major guest appearance, in my dream of owning and running a thriving and just company. Co-dreaming is much more fun.

That someone came along at precisely the right time. On an unseasonably warm October night in 2008, during the early days of the Great Recession, I connected with Jim Pollack, a dear old friend who found his way to DC after years in Tucson. He had always been a landscape and interior designer by trade, and in 2008, those trades were in free fall, right along with the stock market. Jim and I started talking about what came next for both of us. I pitched the idea of property management over a bottle of wine.

"What else do you have?" he asked.

"More wine?" I replied.

I framed the prospect in the most accessible terms. Property management gave the owner (us) the chance to create a great living experience but was also an easy way to make a little side money. That was really my entry point. Every "door" we managed would add up, and each of us, struggling with the looming recession, could lean on management as a hedge against employment uncertainty and a rocky economy.

Plus, what if it *did* turn into something we could scale? I was in heavy sell mode, and before Jim knew what happened to him, our Nest (DC) was in the design phase. For those who know me, it's no surprise that I was all in before I even truly knew what that meant.

One of my earlier side-hustles involved doing wedding videos. I can offer an insider perspective here: Nobody should pursue this line of business (unless all you want is great stories to tell). It was tedious and time-intensive, the hours were terrible, and the pay was crap. Back in the day, the only way to put the videos together was through linear editing. In other words, there was no going back to add something you might have missed or drop in that best man speech you forgot about. There was no room for error, unless you were fine delivering a mediocre video. This was one reason why filmmaking never worked out for me.

I'm a fan of making mistakes and fixing them on the go, of testing ideas and tossing them if the outcomes don't produce the desired results. I don't care to get bogged down in details; I want to see, quickly, whether my ideas have traction. I like getting started on a story before I know just how it is supposed to end. My approach to business offers a perfect option for a non-linear growth trajectory with a lot of room for plot twists and the introduction of new characters.

That philosophy, paired with an unwavering interest in standing out by standing up for what we believe in, was part of Flock's successful blueprint. It was one we drew along the way, a giant eraser by our sides. We built a flock of companies that could change flight paths quickly when our course needed to be corrected. And we did that early and often, leveraging a lean startup framework without realizing what we were up to.

THE LEAN STARTUP

Since I've never considered myself straight, non-linear and iterative business designs come naturally. When our company was a fledgling, we found ourselves informally and instinctively running a lean startup without any vocabulary for that approach. The methodology was groundbreaking despite being, at its core, a basic concept: Keep it simple. It eschewed "big design up front" development and instead relied on targeted, low-investment testing of hypotheses to discover, in real time, whether concepts had legs or needed adjustment. The business plan isn't what comes first in a lean startup. In fact, you might draft it as you go—if you get there at all. This model has teeth in any field, industry, or business no matter the size or where it's positioned in its lifecycle.

A lean startup approach gave us permission to test the waters with our business, study, and better understand our customer, and make adjustments as necessary. Not knowing that this was a best practice, we simply believed it wasn't logical to map our five-year journey if we weren't sure which direction would be most successful. It turned out, we were in good company with this assumption. Startup evangelist Steve Blank, in his article "Why the Lean Start-Up Changes Everything," neatly summed up the difference between established business trajectories and lean startup businesses: "One of the critical differences is that while existing companies *execute* a business model, start-ups *look* for one. This distinction is at the heart of the lean start-up approach. It shapes the lean definition of a start-up: a temporary organization designed to search for a repeatable and scalable business model."[10]

This came naturally for us because a temporary state of being was our standard state of being. We had to flex depending on our client base, customer size, talent, legal and regulatory changes, technology, and system needs that changed constantly. But we found a scalable business tucked neatly within the property management industry, which has substantial growth potential because it is essential. Its poor reputation among consumers and outdated systems were opportunities for us. We found a problem to solve, and we continuously tested our solutions within the industry. Starting small, paying as we went, and having extremely limited resources gave us a natural competitive advantage because we were forced to be focused and economical at once. All that said, lean or not, going into any field with your eyes wide open is critical. And there is a lot to see in the property management space.

Our cheerful approach to problem solving is pretty novel for DC, especially given that the mid-Atlantic region isn't

---

particularly known for its service-forward culture. John F. Kennedy agreed, noting in a 1961 speech, "Somebody once said that Washington was a city of Northern charm and Southern efficiency."[11] But I found myself a welcome house guest when I arrived in DC, and helping friends solve problems in their spaces (read: handyladying) became my thing. Initially, I was floored by the lack of literacy my neighbors and friends had when it came to maintaining, styling, and just basically living in a home. "Did you change the air filter?" I'd ask when folks inquired why their AC broke. "The handle on my toilet doesn't work. Do you have a plumber?" "I have common sense," I thought. Then I'd find myself walking them through the anatomy of a toilet handle chain. Few, if any, in my circle had any exposure to maintaining a space. They were helpless at best and a threat to their very own homes at worst. Those who didn't own were in a constant state of frustration about their lousy landlord, probing me for tips on how landlord-tenant laws work. There were a lot of problems that needed solving among those in my network, and it provided me a good sampling of a client base. This was long before I sold Jim on Nest, but clearly, I had incentives to incubate the idea. During those early District years, I was deep in the nonprofit space but was noticing some common themes.

DC needed a stellar management company that actually maintained spaces, cared about community, and delivered exceptional service. Property management needed a gut renovation, and I had lots of clues as to why. Solving problems

---

[11] Keyes, "Ask Not Where This Quote Came From."

is the hallmark of any startup, and after Flock was started, having a perpetual startup ethos kept us soaring.

Nobody picks up the phone in this business. No wonder it's considered a "phone it in" (or rather, a "don't pick up the phone") industry. If we solved just this one problem, we would be ahead of the game. And answering the phone is free. Yet the trend is unsurprising. I know this because we've been picking the phone up for over a decade. Whoever is on the other end is calling with their own set of problems that need to be solved, and they are counting on you. It's a tough business full of real-time complexity.

It's not a shock the industry's turnover rate is a stunning 36.1%,[12] in contrast with a national average of 25%.[13] There is a difference between lean and full-on understaffed and/or underqualified. This is the operational positioning of most management companies, burning out too few staff. The industry isn't nimble because the profit model doesn't allow for it. Pausing to refine or revise systems is perceived as too costly, and let's be honest, it is time consuming. Staffing with an eye toward experience and quality of life increases expenses and threatens bottom line profits. Never mind the churn. Typical management companies are drowning.

While there are numerous professional credentials and certifications available for the field, most don't go that route until they've settled into the industry, as opposed to learning

---

[12] Home365, "Employee Retention in Property Management."
[13] Glassdoor, "Here's What Your Turnover and Retention Rates Should Look Like."

how to do the work before they get started. Once properties add up, it's a bit like (or a lot like) drinking from a firehose. It is easy to picture the industry's downsides, particularly for those who aren't interested in disrupting anything but are most invested in maximizing their profits. Scale and quality in this scenario are almost impossible to achieve.

But Flock took the long view. Investments early in high quality team members and exceptional client and resident experiences would attract more business. We could (and did) eclipse the industry's natural growth curve by investing in people and systems that allowed us to manage many more properties very well, with evolving, sophisticated tools that changed with our portfolio size rather than collapsing from the pressure of increased volume. We had control over our systems and our talent. This was critical, because much of what we managed day-to-day was unpredictable.

The opportunity for error in real estate management is immeasurable on the client and the resident side. If you don't own the units you manage, you lack a certain amount of agency. We had no capital to acquire real estate, so like most management companies, we handled property on behalf of the client/investor as a third party vendor. Many of these clients/investors were what you might call accidental landlords. They were owners who found themselves with a property they decided to rent vs. sell. Maybe the market was bad, and they were upside-down in the investment; perhaps, they thought they might move back into the unit at some point. Other clients were straightforward investors—the people or groups that invest in a property for the sole purpose of renting it while building equity and, ideally, making a profit year after year and enjoying tax breaks. Every client, how ever they find themselves in this position, is cost sensitive, and most aren't inclined to spend more money than they need to. So, with our commitment to offering dignified, high-quality housing, we were (and still are) in a constant state of selling the value of our approach to our client base and justifying investments in maintaining stellar spaces while offering an outstanding experience for residents and the community. Talk about a hard sell.

But we can empathize with the investor perspective. If, for example, you're moving on from a space you called home and thought was great, it can be hard to hear that all the walls need to be repainted, the carpet is a disaster, and the running toilet, 18-year-old hot water heater, and leaky sink all need to be updated. Today, we can talk to owners about the cost benefit of making investments, even for their tenants. Great spaces attract responsible tenants who take better care of units and stay longer. The upside to those advantages can't be overstated. We can now lean on our track record to illustrate how measurably effective this strategy is. We also can share data on performance, including: repair costs over lease terms; the increase in value over time; vacancy rates; and eviction statistics, which continue to be negligible because they almost never happen in our portfolio—less than ten in 13 years. That data, along with our justice-based values system, makes for a compelling argument.

Now toggle to the resident (tenant) relations side of the work. From tracking residents' basic contact information to having fluency around how each property needs to operate to engaging in the logistical battles that need to be fought to ensure effective maintenance, much of the work is an exercise in professional acrobatics. Factor in the statistical likelihood that the resident is stressed out, inconvenienced, or losing patience, and the potential for a fruitful and fulfilling relationship with your client/resident can plummet before you even meet. All told, management can be like sitting down for a professional test and the best grade available is a C+. Layer in naturally complicated logistics, a 24/7 on-call lifestyle in the early years, and lots of bullies whose expectations are never aligned with reality, and it's easy to see why my industry peers avoid the phone, and in particular, why Jim wasn't an easy sell. He had socializing to do, after all. But the hard parts are easy to imagine and, in my experience, quite predictable. The magic of management, the chance to make a difference and a living at once, is what I was really selling Jim that night.

The management downsides revealed themselves predictably and quickly once we got into the swing of things. Jim wasn't wrong to be skeptical. But my personal experience in management had long scored an A+, and that was what I wanted to replicate. The philosophy and mission we applied was our secret sauce, and I already had proof of concept. By the time Jim and I sat down that October night, I had been caring for about 15 different properties over the previous decade. That would become the first branch in the tree we were nesting in. A few were mine, and I handled some for others. For each unit, I personally coordinated maintenance (or, better yet, performed it myself). Some of the tenants

I don't recall at all, and some I wouldn't share a beer with. But a few ended up working for the company, and a sizable number attended my wedding. I always had a chance to get to know my residents because I was not only managing their homes, but I was also constantly tinkering to improve them or keep them in good repair. A few new exterior light fixtures, a fresh coat of exterior paint, new fencing or trees when the budget allowed, and a roofing ladder I made very good use of had shown that, with my own two hands, I could improve on my assets and my tenants' homes.

Just like we do for clients today, I tried to stay flexible and open-minded and to see making investments in my property as a long game, not short-term cash outlays. That was hard when I wasn't flush, so I needed to be creative about managing my very limited financial resources.

One resident, Justin, wanted to upgrade his backyard with a patio. This made sense. Minus a small deck, the yard was an urban unicorn, measuring 100 feet long and 19 feet wide. It was a bear to maintain, so I liked the idea. I could afford materials for the patio by working with a wholesaler out of town, and I saved delivery expenses using the 1992 blue Toyota beater truck I bought for 600 bucks. I was the only one I knew with a truck in the District, let alone one with a manual transmission. Fortunately, this one had a reverse gear. Justin and I made a deal. If we could do the install together, I could make the patio happen ASAP. Over a three-day weekend, we hauled pavers, spread sand, and tamped and leveled and tamped and leveled until we were ready to finish off the dull, gray 12x12 pavers with a rust patina, using a cheap paint sprayer from Ace Hardware. It was transformational.

We admired our work over well-deserved beers and promised to convene again. Justin wasn't just a tenant, he was a neighbor—and a happy one at that—with a sweet new patio to enjoy.

That yard had been mine at one time. It was my first home in DC and a total disaster. After losing bids on six houses, I made a desperate offer on that hot mess of a house at the last minute, knowing I would soon lose proof of income with an upcoming employment transition. If the house didn't close, I would need to rent. And I had enough of that as a little girl. I wanted a home of my own when I got to Washington. My bid was accepted, and the wild ride of ownership began. I often live in houses and work on them before renting them, but that particular property was barely livable. A flooding basement, leaking roof, windows and doors that didn't close properly, and a lack of working appliances all made that house one of the hardest to call home. Even the yard was a disaster. It was full of broken furniture, construction scraps, appliances, an inoperable dump truck, and typical yard components, like rats and poison ivy. But just like the sweet duplex tucked on a dusty, downtown residential alleyway in Arizona, this DC house helped me build a sense of community while building security for myself. From the residents who also called it home to the village of friends and vendors that helped bring it back to life, I built memories there while others did too.

I'm certain I'm in the minority when I talk about the life-changing experiences I've had managing homes. I often wax nostalgic about all the incredible moments I've had from house to house. I learned how to work with my hands, transform spaces for the better, communicate and connect with residents, collect rent, handle middle-of-the-night frozen pipes, post craigslist ads, and prep a lease. For me, it was all in the intention and the relationship you have with the house and the residents. I was also clever, always choosing houses with more than one unit and living in them. All told, I spent more than 27 years living with my residents, each of us with our own space but, together, making the unaffordable accessible—and, for me, building equity over time.

I only stopped renting a unit in my home in 2020 to make way for family members displaced by the pandemic. I love that this time will be forever memorialized in the 2020 US Census. I imagine generations to come, puzzling over that detail when working with their own version of ancestry.com. That my passion for housing and justice and business created space for that pandemic shelter and delivered security for all of us is a point of pride. I will never take that for granted.

These A+ experiences were my real-life landlandying education. They were not based on credentials and *certainly* not based on refined business models. And these experiences gave me an absolutely bonafide baseline for providing exceptional, justice-based service in the housing world. That's why property management, a business that can scale while doing good, was increasingly attractive to me as a long play. If Jim and I pulled it off, it would also be a chance to build long-term security for myself and for others. I understood then, managing homes was truly my life's work—even if it took me a bit to get there. I was 37 when we started feathering a bonafide Nest (DC, LLC), which would eventually become a Flock family of companies tending to over 5,500 residents.

CHAPTER 5

A PROBLEM
IS AN OPPORTUNITY

H ow our Flock of birds came to be and why our unique approach to designing and running a justice-based business is one very much worth studying because business can and should be an agent of change. As business owners, we can self-elect to pay exceptional wages, tend to the community, and create opportunities for those often left behind because of status or education. We can reduce our environmental footprint and invest profits in people and places instead of hoarding cash for owners and investors. We can create more equity and share the abundance, rather than operate in the scarcity-based mindset popular among traditional capitalists who answer to their shareholders. We now have the advantage of hindsight, which we can pass along to anyone interested in launching or redesigning a business. This story of Flock and our family of birds illustrates how we did it. While I will spend time sharing our story, I also consider it a joy to share the stories of other companies on the justice journey.

Some of the businesses I highlight are relatively new to me, and others are old friends. All of them are inspirational. One of these icons is in my own backyard. While I didn't have a proper business mentor, I was certainly in awe of a few local entrepreneurs. Gina Schaefer, founder and CEO of A Few Cool Hardware Stores, was one of those business crushes. Nest was in its infancy when Gina's was flying high (and it hasn't landed yet). It took years for me to gather the courage to ask her for a networking coffee. I'm glad I did. I've counted Gina as both a close friend and business *shero* ever since. And if you're smart, and I think I am, you keep *sheroes* close at hand.

Gina is a local entrepreneurial legend, who now owns 13 ACE hardware stores in a town once so limited in its home improvement options that Home Depot actually ran out of paint colors and 2" trim brushes. No property manager's tool kit is complete without a trim brush. Gina didn't just fill a marketplace gap, she created good jobs for those being left behind, and she did it while reminding us all that "Main Street" should be the heart of our communities. At the start, a single hardware store was her ambition, and she staffed the store with a ready crew of recovering addicts—paying them above minimum wage and offering a rich benefits package that included healthcare, paid sick time, profit sharing, 401k's, and room for advancement. None of this was or is commonplace in retail, but Gina's company goes well beyond caring for their team. They create neighborhood anchors. Ace offers non-profits 10% off on all purchases, and Gina led the board of Directors for Think Local First, which, since 2006, has "been dedicated to supporting local independent business in our nation's capital." Their "mission is to support responsible local businesses and create the conditions in which they thrive. They thrive in order to make Washington, DC a more vibrant, inclusive and equitable place to live, work and play."

Gina solved that problem, and she did it with a purpose-driven approach to business that's inspired. Gina's industry is also an example of a retail service many of us are consumers of, directly or indirectly, and her approach illustrates how disrupting an industry can be profitable for the owner, the client, the team member, and the community.

She didn't set out to open 13 hardware stores. She thought she'd mount the sign on her Logan Circle location and settle into life as a Main Street businesswoman. But as she tells the story, it was days before customers asked where she would be opening her second or third location. When Gina's company began taking off, she made sure to bring her team with her. As a case in point, she started an employee stock ownership plan in 2021, and she continues to see her team as whole people, rather than assets. Indeed, she sees her team as the future and the owner of the company's success.

Gina's competitor isn't the mom-and-pop shop down the street. It's the dangerous Amazons and Walmarts of the world, with Walmart almost looking like a corner store compared to the magnitude of Amazon's reach today. The danger in supporting the oligopolies and monopolies that are forming over and around us is social, political, cultural, environmental, and economic. It's a threat to freedom and to justice, and while it's being positioned as an abundance of choice, these behemoth corporations are actually eliminating true options by suffocating and killing small businesses by manipulating the marketplace and its pricing. Communities suffer in a fight between elephants. So do many businesses, like local hardware stores. This has global and local repercussions. Justice is at stake when the balance of power in business is so misaligned with community needs. Global businesses cannot tend authentically to local economies and communities. We need home team advantages, and Gina's business is the experienced coach.

CHAPTER 6

THE BUSINESS CASE FOR JUSTICE AND THE JUSTICE CASE FOR BUSINESS

There's no market for a product that doesn't work. Whether you're in the business of advancing social justice as an entrepreneur or not, it's imperative you build a company that delivers an exceptional product or service, like selling hardware where people live and use hardware. In our business, residents and owners want well-cared-for homes, responsive service, a human touch, and the ease of using mobile-optimized apps to reach us. Plus, they want us to answer the phone. They want the very best of a high-touch interface and a hands-off, "set it and forget it" role to play all at once. We deliver.

We knew we were offering a welcome alternative to "phone-it-in management" and, given how many people rent across this country, it remains a problem very much worth solving. According to Housing Wire, RentCafe reported in 2019 that "the renter population had become more than 100 million strong after a decade of sustained growth, as the number of American renters reached 108.5 million in 2018, up from 99.4 million in 2010."[14] These numbers continue to rise, in part, because the rate of homeownership among BIPOC buyers has declined since the great recession—an alarming topic I spend time on at the end of this book. Even if rentals are my bread and butter, home ownership is essential to our country's economic and social well-being and should not be reserved for largely white buyers. This has become a pronounced trend since the Great Recession paired a deficit of five million houses in America with no pathway to owning them for millions of people.

With demand in the rental market showing no signs of slowing down, from where we're perched, we believe that demand should be met with dignified, high-quality housing that is well-managed whether the resident is there for a lease term or a lifetime. That's justice-based management. It's also a tall order. But Flock is up for the job because we care deeply about the outcomes, and we're willing to test industry boundaries and rewrite the rules. During the early years of what

---

[14] Lloyd, Alcynna. "Decade in Review: Number of U.S. Renters Surpasses 100 Million." *HousingWire*, 12 Mar. 2020, https://www.housingwire.com/articles/decade-inreview-number-of-u-s-renters-surpasses-100-million/.

eventually became Flock, we stumbled as often as we caught air, partly because there was no pre-set flight path for us. And that was okay.

We also continue to (re)design our business to solve problems. The problems are the opportunities; they are constantly changing. Your business needs to change with them, and it's why a startup ethos is a formidable solution to a mutable problem set. Every day offers a new opportunity to start again. We are always working to optimize operations for excellence, and we use a lean startup lens when testing new ideas, new products, and new marketing strategies. With those tests, we have the information we need to make radical adjustments to our operations if they will improve results and meet the changing needs of our clients, residents, and community. We make these changes even if they are at a considerable expense.

For example, we've had to onboard and offboard countless communication tools over time. Early in the business, phone communication was preferred among most clients. Later, it became email, then text messages. Now, it is in-app communication. That doesn't mean there aren't still residents who need and appreciate in-person conversation because they don't have email or phones or "in-app" anything, let alone mobility. You have to meet people where they are to serve them well. That means quickly pivoting when our outreach tools are failing to reach the right people the right way at the right time. Even if it is expensive and an enormous amount of work. Because designing the business to serve our stakeholders is an investment in the company and the team that makes it successful.

Whatever tools we're using and no matter the systems we're refining, eliminating, or building, everything we do is driven by our social justice commitment. To be a just business is to be an empathic one. We have to care deeply about serving our clients, our residents, our team, and our community. To be a thriving company is to be one that's delivering excellence and justice at once. Flock can't do one without the other. They are codependent—in a good way.

This is the cycle of home and justice for us: A happy resident calls a well-maintained, safe, and dignified home their own. They settle in, they nest, and they care for their space. That house becomes a cared-for architectural neighbor, preserved for the next home dweller. Happy homes and home dwellers attract more of the same. When our Flock tends to people and places with respect and exceptional service, networks are naturally engaged, and interest is piqued in what we do and how we do it. Our growing business is able to invest in systems that are better, more sophisticated, and relevant. We can build attractive, effervescent brand collateral because it's authentic, engaging, and relatable. We use growing revenues to increase salaries and attract and retain attentive, empathic talent. Our tenure averages are statistically unheard of in the industry, and team members can spend their time with the company working on and in causes that matter to them as part of their work, not in addition to it. Every Flocker can invest volunteer time and cash into critical causes and for marginalized communities. We talk louder for those not listening when we argue and act in favor of equity, humanity, and our environment—and even louder when we rage against racism and injustice. When we do better, we do better. Social justice is the common denominator. It is our engine and our path to profitability and the abundance it offers.

Getting to the business of running a business powered by justice required more than a robust value system. It required an operational foundation—things like a bank account and money to put in it, plus a phone number, a website, and of course, business cards. Luckily, none of that was a tall order when I identified property management as a legitimate business prospect. Since I'd never had an appetite for risk, my passion for real estate management was strengthened by its easy entry point. It didn't require a huge cash investment, and we could deliver evolving solutions to the client's problem with minimal investments outside of our time, creativity, and passion. To build a property management company, the math *is* pretty simple. The website was our most significant cost at the time since pre-packaged sites were both aesthetically unappealing and hard to use. With the business cards, a bit of insurance, a business license, an email address, and a phone line, I figured the monthly costs would be somewhere around $200. That meant we needed to onboard roughly two properties to cover minimum expenses. Things like professional fees, licensure, tools, vehicles, and management software were all off in the distance. Even those costs were relatively minimal, though. Legal Zoom provided us with an operating agreement and helped us form our LLC. All told, we spent around $5,000 for the website and LLC. It's hard to think of a cheaper set up. And I was born to save.

As a kiddo, my mom made a ceramic piggy bank for me. It didn't feature a belly cork, so every deposit I made was there to stay until that pig was in pieces. I loved stuffing that hand-made bank just as much as any other because I didn't see myself ever dipping into those reserves. Eventually that pig hit the ground, and my cash reserve matured. But I'm pretty sure whatever was in there found its way to my current 401k plan. I don't care for risk.

Fortunately, my interest in business didn't have to come at the expense of a stable state of being. Property management is a naturally lean business. It can operate without any substantial financial outlays, which decreased my vulnerability as a business owner and as a human being who grew up feeling so vulnerable I could never really shake the feeling. In property management, I didn't think I had much to lose, and, financially, I didn't. Further, operating a cash business without investors meant I could focus on our non-monetary impact all day long. This gave me room to explore my business as an agent for change and offered a counterpoint to traditional models of profitability. I chose an industry (or an industry chose me) that's reliant on human talent with a focus on meeting the human need for housing. It's an industry with ups and downs for sure, but it has a stability that leaves a lot of breathing room. I didn't need to carry inventory or invest in significant assets or operational building blocks to get started. The smartphone was our mobile office, and other information management tools allowed for streamlined operations and workflows. I didn't need a room of filing cabinets. Almost all our filing happened in the cloud. We reduced the administrative burden as much as possible to keep the work simple and straightforward. We couldn't afford to do it any other way, and that way was filled with trial and error—the ingredients for any effective lean startup and our natural, intuitive approach to the work.

On the error side, I admit, our mistakes and poorly conceived ideas were abundant. And so many of them had to do with keys and cars. For our first few years in business, keys to the buildings and units we managed were stored conveniently in the center console of the company truck. The full-sized, extended cab pickup was nearly impossible to park anywhere in the city, but we assumed if a Nester was at a property, they must have arrived in the truck. That half-baked idea lasted an embarrassingly long time, as did the truck. Gina shared a similar story. It took more than a year before she realized they should count the cash in the register at the end of the night. Turns out, to them, it was a big change drawer. Eventually, she figured it out. We did too. When the truck stopped performing well as key storage, we moved the keys. (Here's some industry-insider info: more keys, more problems. I did an interview a few years ago and was asked what one of our biggest challenges had been over the decade. I had a one word answer: keys. If I really want to get rich, I'll solve the global key problem.) Truth be told, for a while, the truck worked really well as key storage because we only had a handful of keys. But business needs to evolve and be highly responsive not only to market shifts but also to the environment (social, political, economic, and natural); client base demographics and needs; generational shifts; staffing and culture needs; and, finally, the needs of your community, however you choose to define it. When you work this way, you create an opportunity for the business/justice/business cycle to continue. Good business gets more good business. The opposing model lacks impact and undermines profit potential.

PART THREE

CHAPTER 7

FOREVER STARTING

Steve Blank established himself as an expert in early-stage companies when he coined the term "startup," which he defines in part as, "an organization formed to search for a repeatable and scalable business model."[15] Another high profile entrepreneur, WhatsApp co-founder Jan Koum, said, "a startup is a feeling."[16] For us, being a startup meant we were solving an obvious problem in our corner of the marketplace, and our point of reference was our existing competition and their likely unhappy client base. The Y Combinator is a famous, early-stage business incubator in Mountain View, California, that has helped launch more than 2,000 startups, including Airbnb, DoorDash, Reddit, and DropBox.

---

[15] Blank, "Why the Lean Startup Changes Everything."
[16] Balova, "Should 10-Year-Old Companies Call Themselves Startups."

Jared Friedman, a partner at Y Combinator, makes the point that the startup ethos isn't about coming up with an entirely new product or service. In fact, it may be that you simply deliver a better solution in an existing market. Friedman says, "You should actually err on the side of doing things with existing competitors. When founders go into spaces with no existing competitors, they usually find out that the reason there are no competitors is because nobody wants the product. The ideal situation is a market where there are existing competitors, but you have noticed something that they all seem to have missed."[17] Traditional property management was missing the whole point. That performance chasm has been the driver of our success in a vulnerable industry. We were in good company among other startups. According to Forbes, "Startups are young companies founded to develop a unique product or service, bring it to market and make it irresistible and irreplaceable for customers." Startups are rooted in innovation, addressing the deficiencies of existing products or creating entirely new categories of goods and services, thereby disrupting entrenched ways of thinking and doing business for entire industries. That's why many startups are known within their respective industries as "disruptors."[18]

Industries can change. Though I haven't seen much of that in property management, which has been stubbornly static, we've all learned by now, every industry can be reinvented,

---

[17] Friedman, "How to Get Startup Ideas: Startup Ideas, Problems to Solve, Becoming a Founder: Y Combinator."

[18] Baldridge, "What Is a Startup?"

property management included. Look at service behemoths like car insurance and banking. Both have radically transformed over the last 30 years despite offering essentially the same product from start to finish. And oftentimes, when one industry improves, it leaves room for others to as well. Telecommunications is a prime example.

My grandparents had a party line on their farm in Colorado—not the kind with a 1-900 number, but the kind you shared with neighbors down the road. When we picked up the wall-mounted rotary phone, if we heard someone from down the road, say the Nelson family, on the line, we checked back later. In a pinch, you could take the Jeep for a quick five minute run to Hygiene, Colorado, where the convenience store had a behind-the-counter phone for locals. None of this was unusual to me. In Hailey, there were so few folks and so few phones, we only needed the last four digits to call out. It was a major adjustment when a prefix came into my life, let alone when I later had to memorize area codes. Periodically, the family made a trip to the phone store. Prior to the 1980s, you didn't own your phone, you leased it. That was before the antitrust lawsuit against AT&T was finalized in 1982, breaking up the monopoly of the Bell System into the "Baby Bells." Up until that point, AT&T held an unfair monopoly with sole control of North America's entire communication system. On top of having to lease the phone, customers also had to pay a Bell Systems technician to come to their house, install a phone jack, and plug the phone into the wall, where it was affixed permanently. There were no other options for consumers. After the monopoly was broken up, companies like Sprint and

MCI emerged, giving us more choices and, unfortunately, a complex and consumer-unfriendly oligopoly.

What, to date, has disrupted the property management industry? Aside from smartphones, a few new players in property management technology, and some advances in federal policy, like fair housing, not much in the industry has changed for decades in terms of service delivery. We would have noticed if the industry had been transformed. Consumers haven't realized it needs to, or maybe they have resigned themselves to accepting its mediocrity.

Consumers still, for all the choices and power we have today, regularly accept mediocre products, systems, or services because we don't have options. That has historically been the case with eyeglasses, their inflated costs, their long turnaround times, and all the surprise "extras" that add up so quickly. Buying glasses can feel like buying a car, and buying cars has traditionally been terrible. It can take an entire day for no reason beyond haggling over prepaid maintenance programs and unnecessary clear coats. Similarly, we have accepted that property management is a broken industry that can take its consumers for granted. The same can be said of the mattress racket, where super sales are so frequent, you have to wonder if there even is a base price at all? All of these static, stale, and somewhat shady industries create entirely new opportunities for disruption and a different kind of customer choice. I'm talking about Warby Parker, Casper, VROOM, and Avocado Green Mattresses. By operating at the margin of an industry, they aren't bogged down with brick-and-mortar expenses and long-term obligations, like the dreaded 5–10–15-year commercial lease.

These companies can operate as lean startups, testing new products or hypotheses quickly to refine, focus, and eliminate error (costs) and increase growth and market share (income). These novel companies are finding ways to be operationally competitive with Amazon by cutting out the middle person and going direct to the consumer.

Stacey Price is a local icon and retail *shero* who has taken the concept of local commerce and recast a business model that benefits the community, makers, and the economy. Today, Stacey is the brain and the brawn behind Made in DC, a cooperative retail model that aggregates the work of local makers in shops with high pedestrian visibility. The stores host workshops, bring together artisans, offer gathering spaces, and expand visibility and credibility for a community of entrepreneurs who would otherwise be fighting their way through the increasing noise of Etsy and those who couldn't afford the opportunity costs that eclipsed earning potential by entering the traditional retail marketplace—if there is such a thing these days.

Zooming with Stacey for this book, it was a thrill to think back on the arc of our relationship as local business women. I was lucky to cross paths with Stacey when she was head of the DC Think Local First chapter. Her passion for local business, creative arts, and retail was intoxicating. With a head of red hair and a smile a mile wide, she lit up every room she entered, and I was lucky enough to call her a mentor and coach as I began to imagine a bigger, more impactful future for myself and my growing businesses. When she logged onto our video call she was breathless, suffering a sudden staffing snafu, burning out as we all do. But Stacey understands deeply she has a model that might just be the future of local retail on a national level. I felt lucky to get the time with her because everybody wants her magic formula. Since launching Made in DC in 2017, she has expanded to seven stores and has requests from communities across the country to open regionally focused outlets. She feels the pressure, but she understands the promise her vision offers. She doesn't measure success in profit, but instead, she measures her success in the local dollars she's generated for makers selling through her stores. As of this writing, that number is six million dollars and counting. The potential impact is inspired, and the cooperative model reduces risk and increases opportunity at the same time. This is purpose driven business at its very best. Stacey is creating an entirely new category for retail, and the buyer has been pleased. So has the city.

Like Stacey, we wanted to redefine things in the home management industry, things that everyone took advantage of or for granted. Our key competitive advantage has been our delivery of a high-touch service, quality homes, and a purpose-driven ethos—everything our industry isn't known for. We had a hunch there was a strong consumer base for our unique management approach. Consumers weren't just interested in our model, though; they were enthusiastic fans once they understood they did indeed have a choice.

We know, from both a consumer and a competitor perspective, our competition can deliver baseline service for tenants and property owners when the company is run well enough. Generally (and observationally) speaking, the industry lacks compassion, empathy, and an appreciation for the magnitude of its responsibilities. After thirteen non-stop years in the field, I can say property management as a practice doesn't operate with enough commitment to service to improve the field. And there is little incentive within the industry to ameliorate the problem when mediocrity sets the bar. Management companies are competing for business and contracts, but it's rare to see our peers in the field try to outperform anything other than our pricing. The contracts in the industry are sticky; in other words, it's a pain to switch management companies, and most renters, once they are situated in their spaces, are more or less bound to the lease terms and lack much consumer agency. Given this paradigm, there isn't much incentive for a traditional management company to refine systems, improve service, or even stand out if there are enough contracts and profits to justify the current state of being and operation. The business, even at its worst, is a stable one. The traditional management refrain might be "you win some you lose some" when it comes to contracts or "if it's not broken" (when it very clearly is) or, my personal least favorite, "it's just a rental."

That's not Flock.

We are disruptive to the industry because we care the most and treat houses like homes and tenants like residents and neighbors. This is a more just approach to management, which gives us an advantage because we can openly address gaps in the existing industry standards and procedures.

We're able to call out the industry for poorly-maintained or unhealthy houses, its lack of responsiveness, blatant fair housing violations, inflated prices, year-over-year increase, and the threat of the unit being suddenly sold or eventually unaffordable or unlivable. That's not right. And yet both the industry and investors often feel justified in putting residents' needs last when calculating the value of the asset. Management companies can defer maintenance, use substandard materials, have a lack of responsiveness in emergencies, and blame tenants for anything broken. In many cases, owners align with management companies to reduce costs and increase income on every property. This is not an unreasonable aim, but in this very human industry with the fabric of communities (made up of people and housing) in the balance, this simple formula can have very complex costs. Poorly maintained homes lead to communities that are more fragile. It's easy to see that this is a self-perpetuating business model because it's a profitable one. In his book *Evicted, Poverty and Profit in The American City*, Matthew Desmond reports the stunningly tragic stories of families trying to outrun eviction and the landlords on their heels in Michigan. He writes, "We have failed to fully appreciate how deeply housing is implicated in the creation of poverty. Not everyone living in a distressed neighborhood is associated with gang members, parole officers, employers, social workers, or pastors. But nearly all of them have a landlord."[19]

---

[19] Desmond, *Evicted: Poverty and Profit in the American City*, 5.

At their worst, property management companies prey on and profit from those experiencing housing insecurity, and those with limited choices pay more when management companies let repairs go unmade, escalate rent as early and as often as possible, and hold residents responsible for what should typically be handled by the owner, including basics like plumbing. Certainly, not every management company can be swept into the same category of predatory landlords, but most of us are failing to understand or appreciate the magnitude of our responsibility to provide dignified housing. This focus is almost always left out of the conversation in favor of the economics and risk/reward dynamics of the industry. As a values-based company, Flock's service stands in stark contrast to these management models. We're solving problems at a human level vs. the simple bottom line approach taken industry-wide.

What problem does Flock solve that others cannot or choose not to? We are very, very good at managing real estate because our approach is holistic. We care for the property, the resident, the client, and the community, rather than pitting one against the other. We're not interested in a zero-sum game and believe everyone wins when property is well managed. We deploy empathy as a strategy. We maintain homes as if they are our own and with the highest possible standards. When things begin to fail, we act quickly, from broken air conditioners to basement restorations after a flood. We respond quickly to middle-of-the-night phone calls when there are leaks and lockouts. We manage the complex legal and financial requirements for our clients and take good care of residents and our community. Flock is a service-forward, high-touch company in a market that rarely demonstrates this (differentiating) characteristic. We solve problems cheerfully, even though they are abundant in our business. To do so, we lean back on technology while leaning into the very personal nature of the resident experience. We don't look for short-cuts. We look for operational efficiencies, train our talent, and create workflows that make sense. When they stop working, we start over. And we have cultivated attractive brands that honor our social justice values and appeal to an engaged and aligned client base. Consequently, people want to see us succeed and are genuinely rooting for us. We're rooting for them, too. We want to come out and greet our clients and residents because, after all, we're neighbors.

With such a successful business ethos, how are we still outliers in this belief system? Because what's intuitive to us, because of our justice lens, is novel to most. We regularly cross paths with owners and investors who focus exclusively on margins, cap rates and cash flow, and reducing expenses. Sometimes, they sneak into our client base. A few years into the work, we signed a contract with a couple heading back to the Midwest to be near family. They had a nice row home off of North Capital, that famous boulevard you see in openings of political dramas. The property checked all the renovation boxes—open floor plan, tall ceilings, granite countertops, stainless appliances, a yard, and nicely appointed kitchen. It was a sweet house, even if it was like all the others in the category. The location wasn't walkable, and crime wasn't uncommon in the area. Unfortunately, the residents had their house robbed, and electronics and guitars were stolen. We reached out to the owners, requesting an alarm system the tenants were willing to split the bill for. We went back and forth, back and forth. The only thing the owners offered was to have an ADT sticker sent to the house, then they explicitly forbade the installation of an alarm system. After that, I explicitly let them know they needed another management company.

I don't care to work with anyone unwilling to invest in a resident's peace of mind. Unfortunately, what we experienced was par for the course, even in a progressive city where one might assume empathy could eclipse profits in certain circumstances. Being clear about our social justice mission and our core values ensures we are working with owners, residents, vendors, and other stakeholders who can align with our business model. We believe management with social justice leads to better and more profitable outcomes for all. The best part? Leading with values doesn't have to be a more expensive proposition. Our fee structure isn't any more or less expensive than other management companies in the region. What we do require is high standards for housing. While the cost of our services may be on par with that of any management company, our insistence on housing that meets the highest possible standards IS more expensive—in the short term. We partner with the owners and residents to deliver a great service while improving home values, caring for the community and setting residents up for a higher quality of life. Justice relies on the abundance mindset, and that's precisely why we focus first on people and place before profit, and attract partners interested in the same. If it's all about money then agency, trust and impact are sidelined or byproducts, at best. We're not okay with that, and we're in good company.

If homes knit together a property management company, growers certainly thread the floral industry together. Christina Stembel, the founder, CEO, and self-described "Gruntswoman" of Farmgirl Flowers[20] had those growers in mind when she observed the chasm in the floral industry.

Floral retail networks can often operate at the consumer's expense because they drain resources and slow systems down with international shipping and exclusively price-driven procurement—even if efficiency and waste hang in the balance. Dated, wasteful, and overly complicated, the floral industry isn't friendly to growers, buyers, the environment, or flowers for that matter. As consumers, we have accepted clunky, awkward online ordering, too many mediocre, expensive choices, and over-the-top pricing. Lucky recipients are left with cheap, scalloped glass vases, like the ones under your sink right now. And yet, seemingly out of nowhere, things started to brighten for all the stakeholders, thanks to Farmgirl Flowers. I'm Farmgirl's biggest fan(girl) because, like me, Christina is self-made and got her pedigree from country living, not business school. Christina self-elects to advance just causes, and her product is empirically gorgeous, simple, and more sustainable.

---

[20] Decker, "Farmgirl Flowers: A Blooming Startup That Is Disrupting the Flower Industry."

Successful startups are the ones that solve problems or disrupt flawed systems with a better product or a smarter way of operating. Often these problems are annoyances in customer service or waste in production that most of us rage about internally but never dream of actually fixing. That's exactly the theory Christina was testing. Before she launched her California-based 32 million dollar floral company, she felt these annoyances when she purchased over-priced, wilted flowers for delivery to her mother. Christina had worked in the event-planning industry and knew that there were deeply embedded problems in the American floral market. Specifically, bouquets were expensive and often arrived sad and wilted, way too many harmful chemicals were used in the production of flowers, and 40% of all cut flowers never made it into an arrangement and were discarded in florist shops. A 1991 US trade agreement with South American countries removed the tariffs on cut flowers, reducing the price of imported flowers and making it impossible for American flower farmers to compete. In fact, this forced 50% of flower growers in the US out of business. When Christina started Farmgirl Flowers, 80% of flowers were imported into America, with most transported in temperature-controlled aircrafts from thousands of miles away, creating Sasquatch-sized carbon footprints. Early investors told her buying flowers grown domestically, specifically in California, just a few miles from her offices and customers in San Francisco, was a bad business move. But she moved forward. In 2010, Christina quit her full time job as an event planner and started Farmgirl Flowers with the $48,000 she had in her savings account. She differentiated her products by opting for the "Costco approach,"[21] and rather than offering an endless number of options, she offered her customers a limited number of stylish, seasonal bouquets. She wrapped their selections in recycled burlap from coffee bean bags, and purchasers could move on with their days knowing they've brightened someone else's. Christina built a wildly successful company by occupying that perfect intersection between the floral industry and justice, seeing the profitability in doing good business, rather than focusing only on what was good for the bottom line.

As when I started Flock, from the get-go, Christina was committed to building a socially-conscious, integrity-driven company and wanted to "do good in the world." Business advisors and potential investors encouraged her to save money by hiring contractors, rather than employees, but creating good jobs was more important to her. Today everyone who works at Farmgirl Flowers is an employee with benefits. Christina also takes on the injustice women business leaders face. She told *Forbes* magazine that "trying to raise startup money as a female founder was impossible," and even though 78% of flowers are purchased by women for other women, 100% of floral startup investment money was going to businesses run by men. She says she's fortunate now to be part of a tight network of women founders, and she goes out of her way to give priority to women-run businesses. Farmgirl Flowers gives back to women in other ways, too, and in February

---

[21] Decker, "Farmgirl Flowers: A Blooming Startup That Is Disrupting the Flower Industry."

of 2021, they donated ten dollars from each of their "With Heart" bouquets to Planned Parenthood.[22]

In terms of service, Farmgirl does what every other flower-styling and delivery company has been doing for decades: delivering flowers. But her mission to deliver elegant arrangements with a lighter footprint allows her to creatively rearrange a wilted industry. For more than 100 years, the nation had seen a transition away from local florists to national flower networks, like 1–800 Flowers and other competitors of the ubiquitous century-old FTD floral empire. But the fundamental formula remained the same, down to the bud vases and baby's breath. Consumers weren't even asking for anything different, and we accepted the industry "as is." But "as is" isn't so great once you've seen the alternatives.

The best consumer problems to solve are the ones we didn't realize were a problem in the first place. Ideally, you can take an industry by surprise when you solve its customer's problems. That's the definition of disruption, and Farmgirl did just that with a fresh approach to the industry, including the service, the client, the planet, and the community. Christina has tailored her company to be a good steward and advocate for anyone intersecting with the industry. Her approach likely created new demand. She has designed a streamlined, simplified platform, and her procurement is socially and environmentally progressive compared to her peers. Buying a bouquet from Farmgirl is a simple transaction, and simplified

---

[22] Decker, "Farmgirl Flowers: A Blooming Startup That Is Disrupting the Flower Industry."

transactions lead to more simplified transactions. As a heavy Venmo, Zelle, and Apple Pay user, I know we can all agree it's easier when you don't have to pull out your wallet. With FGF, the icing on the easy transaction is choosing to support a just and progressive business that puts people and the planet first. Plus, using that Costco model, Christina curates beautiful arrangements but limits her selection. She limits noise and our tendency as consumers to get over stimulated and just abandon the purchase. Limiting choices makes decisions much easier for consumers.

We believed our own fresh approach to a stale industry could lead to more business. Property management services and companies have never been in short supply in our region. There has always been plenty of consumer choice, but we thought if we stood up for justice and delivered a high-touch, best-in-class service, the competition would be rendered a non-threat. We were right. Over the 12 years after we started, we launched four different companies, and we aggregated nearly seven million dollars in annual gross (pre costs of goods sold) revenue. Our staff of 70+ Flocksters are currently managing more than two billion dollars in residential and commercial real estate throughout the Washington, DC proper. Along the way, we've cultivated a reputation as a forward-thinking, politically-oriented company that hasn't just disrupted the industry but has almost disregarded it altogether in favor of our own corporate culture, values system, and definition of success. The journey has been as dramatic as the industry itself, and I can say quite confidently that I wouldn't change a thing—because even the failures led to success.

What will your story be? Which companies will you root for? As I mentioned earlier, our approach can be applied to any type of business, whether it's a service-based company or one that makes widgets or sends gorgeous, burlap-wrapped bouquets. Further down, I elaborate on the three reasons property management made good business sense for my particular set of circumstances, and I hope this can help shape sound reasoning for self-electing and advancing socially-just companies.

Business strategies aside, though, I can't help mentioning just how satisfying it is for a kid who spent her formative years longing for stable and secure housing to grow up to provide that very support for others. For any of us interested in studying our past to understand our present, it's a rewarding journey, particularly when you can use your losses to generate gains for others. That's my win in business. It always will be.

Christina, Gina, and I came from small towns in red states that don't tend to turn out progressive women CEOs. But here we all are, poking holes in long-established traditional industries to make way, not only for more success for ourselves, but for more impact on our communities, consumer bases, and partners. We're self-taught, self-directed, and self-disciplined. Most importantly, we all self-elected to use our businesses to challenge a status quo that's dependent upon a scarcity paradigm—a function of binary thinking that leads to the haves and have nots. It assumes profits are carved out for a few. We have dismissed long-held assumptions that profit is the singular purpose for any business and turned this binary thinking around. We believe everyone profits with an abundance mindset.

To operate this way, you have to be intentional and run a well-designed business, however iterative it needs to be. I confess, I lacked appreciation for the complexity of the work, including the regulatory, financial, and logistical nuances. I have true respect for all management companies that keep the plates spinning and stay above water. Managing at any kind of scale can be hard as hell. Fortunately, I like winging it, or I wouldn't be writing this book. I'm certain my early management approaches were ethical but probably operationally questionable at best. I tended not to concern myself with those details and instead focused on my good intentions for the win. Ultimately, my lack of real background in the business I was proposing to Jim in the fall of 2008 was a good thing. Had I known more, I wouldn't be in this business at all or living a life of abundance or writing this book. Although I don't recommend it to others as a sound strategy (hence this book), my "winging it" business philosophy and deep determination did a nice job of keeping reality at bay and ambition front and center for me. Plus, my gut told me that delivering property management with a sense of pride, passion, and justice would be a winning bet paired with my experience managing homes on my own. Just as one might have a natural aptitude for learning a language, I have an aptitude for home management. And we all know you don't just wake up one day speaking Spanish—it takes hard work and grit, no matter your natural abilities. That fluency would come for me.

Home management and justice, for me, have always gone hand in hand. But I had a lot of learning to do when it came to business fundamentals. Outside of my auto-renew subscription to *Inc. Magazine*, inhaling of business books, and an unnatural armchair interest in business, I had no professional frame of reference for how a company might work. I didn't know how to create a spreadsheet, file for a business license, open up a corporate bank account, or form a partnership agreement. From budget management and oversight to staffing, compliance, risk management, marketing, data management, contracts and agreements, and more, I was completely in the dark. So was Jim. Candidly, so were the other team members I brought on board over time. My "business" as a property manager at that point was a matter of filling out a schedule C tax form and stuffing receipts into an envelope to snag helpful tax deductions. But that lack of education left a lot of room to be creative and intuitive at once, to do things without being bogged down in the traditional business of running a business. We had room and naivety to test the assumption that business could be an agent of change because we weren't burdened with industry bad practices.

I hope this story can be particularly helpful to those who don't have the "advantage" of a business education or background. I didn't try to get too deep with the work because it was too overwhelming. I started with a basic business check-list, like one you might find in *Inc. Magazine*. Perhaps, the title was "Three Easy Steps to Starting a Million Dollar Company." To simplify my understanding of the property management industry and pursue the work, I honed in on three key, very attractive, simple business advantages property management as a field offered:

1) It has a low-to no-cost operational model and an opportunity to pay as you grow without making significant cash/ capital investments. (In other words, there were no investor risks and more time to focus on the work vs. raising cash.)
2) I had landladying experience, which cultivated my respect for homes, their residents, and the tradespeople that maintained them.
3) Everyone needs housing.

As a social justice entrepreneur, I believe everyone *deserves* housing. Add this values system to the impressive stability of the industry, and profitability seemed well within reach. This was a business I wanted to be in even though it was incredibly hard to do well. Our startup was born, and we arrived without the industry baggage that bogs it down. We've been able to stay in social justice/entrepreneurial startup mode ever since, learning to leverage our position at the margins of the industry to be more attractive and innovative, to make (and learn from) more mistakes, and to switch gears quickly, so that the company could soar.

CHAPTER 8

METHOD TO THE MADNESS

For quite a while, in those early days, we were office squatters. I struck a deal with a former boss, and she agreed not only to keep me employed as I grew another enterprise, but, since she liked having me close by, to also let us operate out of the same offices. There was ample room and after all, it was just me and Jim. We took up every cubic inch of that office space with an intern here and a maintenance tech there. Suddenly, we had a few full-time employees, yet we still managed to get in and out of the parking garage without paying (although it required a constant roundtrip for whoever had the garage fob). It was the best lease I never signed.

One day I announced with authority, we needed to take our money out of Wells Fargo. The local bank branch had no idea who we were. I wanted to bank locally. Every dollar we spent or saved was a vote, and I intended to vote with my conscience. Plus, it seemed to me, a solid banking partner might come in handy if we ever needed anything— like a loan. I got a referral for a relationship manager from a mid-sized regional bank with a decent banking footprint. Jenny came by to visit our offices. She was polished, professional, and confused. At that time, we had anywhere from 4-9 people stuffed into 600 square feet. Phones rang off the hook. Whoever answered the call was responsible for whatever unfolded during the conversation. This was a terrible system, but it was the only way we could make it work. We didn't have enough business or people to create departments or divide tasks or even create predictable workflows.

Even though we barely had room to breathe in our "offices," we felt having an overstuffed couch was a reasonable use of space, even if it actually only provided seating for the dog and one person with a laptop. The only meeting space for our meet up with Jenny featured the sofa. We thoughtfully offered a beverage while she settled in. She leaned forward to grab the glass, and the dog wedged himself behind her like taco filling. "No problem at all!" she said, like we were big business fish. All these years later, I'm close with Jenny both personally and professionally. She's not a dog person, but she is a great banker and an extraordinary person.

In those offices, we started to form a bonafide company. Once we had some of the business basics covered (like a business license and a key storage box in a non-mobile location), we were intentionally lean, focusing on what problem in the marketplace we could solve at the moment. We were always open to changing our model and fine-tuning our approach to delivering the work.

As any company scales, whether justice-based or not, the work changes substantially as the client base increases and the complexity of the business grows. We understood early that managing a handful of properties, as I had done almost on the fly, was an entirely different proposition than managing 50, 100, and later thousands of rentals. But we were thoughtful and intentional about how we met that growth head on, and our methods were straightforward. I think no matter the growth trajectory, any company and/or leader can self-elect and position themselves for measurable impact and profitability at once.

I have since organized the nebulousness of our startup ethos into a handful of basic strategies and am happy to share them, along with the lessons I learned. A lean startup model (as we discovered after the fact) has served us well. The approaches we privileged and the core values we implemented to thrive include:

- Being nimble and open to change
- Managing risk
- Having resilience
- Trusting in talent
- Letting go
- Optimizing operations
- Having an intentional culture

BEING NIMBLE AND OPEN TO CHANGE

The willingness (and commitment) to testing strategies and hypotheses meant we could be agile and ensured we were always solving the right market problem. It didn't much matter that the keys were in the truck, as long as we serviced the client well. Provided we were committed to refining the work, the ugly back office errors and patchwork systems were irrelevant. They were temporary in fact, because every strategy would ultimately be responsive to what we were learning about our client base, our residents, our community, and our competition. And those findings would always be shifting. Our flexibility and ability to accommodate an evolving environment was a strong counterpoint to a stale industry.

Even now, we are eager to try new things but readily abandon them if they don't take flight. When we find a smarter, better, faster way to do something, we start as quickly as we can, no matter how much we invested in the old way. This approach takes practice and surprising discipline, but we started from the beginning and baked it into our culture.

I was early to the startup scene. My first legitimate business unfolded in the backyard shed of the first house my family was able to buy on 2nd Street. Our little American Dream was situated just a few blocks from the retail corridor of Hailey, featuring the majestic art deco Liberty Theater, well past her prime as a sleepy, last-run movie theater. The house was technically a one-bedroom with a lot of additions that had been tacked on over the years. I had the bedroom. My brother took the basement, which didn't have any proper means of egress or any kind of window. My parents slept in what was likely intended to be the dining room and didn't have a door. They used a wooden screen for privacy. I remember it being small, cold, and semi-livable. My stepfather had a desk jammed in between storage shelves and the washer/dryer. But the property did have a number of outbuildings and a great yard. And with those features, I saw an abundance of opportunity.

The house suffered from a lack of planning, a bit of neglect, and a lot of bad design choices. Since we weren't positioned financially or otherwise to hire anyone to make upgrades or changes to the home, all the work done on our house was performed by my stepfather with an assist from my mother or a neighbor. I had no idea how useful this experience would eventually become, but being exposed to a DIY environment was profoundly beneficial for me when I got into property management. Even as a kid, I liked how tactical home repair was. I appreciated the immediacy of improving something, of imagining possibilities instead of taking anything at face value. Because the house and our lives needed some solutions, it gave me the confidence to solve problems. It's true, of course, that a one-bedroom house for a family of four wasn't practical. Still, an addition here and an improvement there offered an example of agency. I saw a brighter future with ownership. Renting could create a lifetime of instability no matter how many bedrooms there were. I'd rather own small than rent big.

When we settled on 2nd, my brother claimed the treehouse, and Mom took pity on me, offering up half the ramshackle garden tool shed to do with what I pleased. What I pleased was to set up my enterprise, The Sherlock Holmes Detective Agency. I didn't find this name the least bit unoriginal. I was in the fourth grade and had just learned to read. Changing schools so often meant a lot of the basics had fallen through the cracks of my patchwork education. At this point, although I'd read all the *Nancy Drew* mysteries I could find, I had an uneasy grasp on what the work of a nonfiction detective entailed. Nonetheless, I had a very clear picture of myself sitting behind my desk and taking meetings with distraught clients to review the scope of their mysteries.

Building a home office in a toolshed isn't very tricky. Given the house was in a perpetual state of repair, construction scraps were at my disposal. I propped some leftover drywall against the walls of the shed, painted it with the dregs of some yellow paint, and finished up with some carpet we had pulled out of the waterlogged basement. I finished it up by dragging in a junky table that worked as a desk.

To land my first client I needed a marketing campaign. I rode my bike to the offices of the local newspaper to take out an advertisement. I remember Roberta, the editor and sole employee of the *Idaho Mountain Express*, as a kind woman who seemed delighted with the plan. Roberta put a free ad in the paper for me. She helped me keep my startup costs low, and I was very appreciative because, logically, I was saving for business cards, which I was sure would be needed down the line. The paper came out every two weeks. I eagerly awaited a rush of business, but as it turned out, there were no mysteries that needed solving. The real issue with my Sherlock Holmes Detective Agency? I definitely wasn't solving a market problem. Even if there were mysteries in need of a solution, a third-party detective service wasn't in demand in Hailey, Idaho. I had misjudged the market. (Nancy had made it look like mystery solving was an essential business.) No matter. I was on to new ideas in an instant.

I was busy cultivating skills that would help me as I pursued more lucrative ideas. Just like I abandoned my dreams of breaking records on the pogo stick when there wasn't a big check in it, I moved on from my Sherlock Holmes Detective Agency and pursued a dozen other ambitious hustles. Some were flops. Some stuck. I learned a lot, whether they succeeded or not. I could have been called a serial (side-hustle) entrepreneur, and I think many startup founders have that in common. We keep working until we're solving the right problem. When I made my way to property management, the problems were abundant.

There are few tenants among us who don't think the industry writ large needs some solutions because residents and owners don't usually solve their own problems. I enjoy solving problems cheerfully, so it's no wonder it's a core value for Flock. Our success depends on our responsive approach to an evolving problem. This includes problems not just in the units themselves or in the industry, but also in the size of our portfolio.

Early on, it was pretty easy to deliver a justice-based, highly-customized management experience for a grand total of 15 units. A 15:1 client to manager ratio favored the client hands down, and I could always be hyper-responsive. Sometimes that even meant caring for my residents' pets when they were away because, well, why not?

Getting to—and pleasing—hundreds and then thousands of residents was a different proposition. But our lack of formal experience and minimal resources gave us an advantage.

They made it easier to deploy a lean startup methodology, even though we were doing it instinctively, because we didn't have an interest in replicating traditional property management models. We had to challenge industry assumptions, test new methods, and find more effective, service-forward solutions as we made our way to a community of 5,500 residents. So we focused on simplicity and offered solutions, like picking up the phone vs. silencing it. And anyone would agree picking up the phone is truly a competitive advantage.

One of the earliest rentals we managed was a small, subterranean, one-bedroom basement unit in a convenient location. The owners paid us to buff out the unit with new flooring, counters, paint, and more. Before long, we were handing the keys over to and welcoming home a lovely couple just moving in together. When we left them to get settled, Jim and I assumed it was a job well done and we could enjoy a stress-free, month-over-month revenue stream, just as we planned that night on the porch six months earlier. What could go wrong once tenants settled in? This was pretty naive, especially for someone with landladying experience. Jim and I were avoiding planning ahead and just plain failing to plan at all because the future was daunting and hard to visualize at the same time. We were building a property management prototype, or what Eric Reis, author of *The Lean Startup*, a veritable business bible, might call a MVP—a minimally viable product.[23] We were choosing not to solve problems we hadn't yet faced,

---

[23] Ries, *The Lean Startup: How Today's Entrepreneurs Use Continuous Innovation to Create Redically Successful Businesses.*

in part because we weren't sure what shape those problems would take or when they might emerge. Provided we had talent on hand, a cheerful approach to problem solving, and a client-centric approach, we figured we would frame up the business as we moved into it.

When my wife and I were prepping our son, Beckett, for preschool, we couldn't fathom our kiddo navigating a day without us. We were shocked when he enthusiastically joined hands with the counselor on the first morning, turning with a smile and a wave like he'd been on his way through that front door a million times. That night we showered him with praise and looked forward to an easy drop off the following morning. When the next morning was a rinse and repeat of the previous day, Beckett suddenly realized that school wasn't a one day event. He had checked it off his bucket list. And worse, he exhausted his bravery reserves on the first day. It took quite a while for him to recover from the shock of regularly-scheduled school and get comfortably settled in.

Just like school is a long-term proposition, good property management doesn't have a "set it and forget it" stage—particularly not in this region. In my early landladying years, I had the luxury of managing property in a dry climate. Water is the number one enemy of housing, and while Tucson is unforgivingly and relentlessly hot, the elements aren't as harsh on housing. When I got to DC, water was housing enemy #1. I hadn't appreciated how much simpler it was to manage less-expensive rentals in a climate that's fairly forgiving. (The cost of living in Arizona is substantially lower.)

My first all-nighter with water in the District was memorable. Right around three am, tucked in my bed on a cool night in March, my phone was suddenly ablaze with urgent messages from our residents, as was Jim's. It was the same charming couple we had welcomed to their new subterranean home a few months earlier. When we reached them by phone, they patiently explained there was quite a bit of water coming into their unit from above. "Hold on a sec," they said. "Just listen as we hold the phone out." It sounded like a fountain. Jim and I were onsite within thirty minutes with buckets, towels, and a good attitude. Each of us had the building management company on speed dial, but with no luck. Without their response, getting the water turned off was tricky, at best. We advised the tenants to grab the dog, the wedding dress (congrats on the engagement!), invitations, and anything else that was irreplaceable if it were to get wet. Then we hooked them up with a pet-friendly hotel about 12 blocks away. We told them not to worry; we had the credit card on file, and they should be able to check in without any headaches. Fast forward a few hours. There was still no assistance from building management. We called the fire department. Axes thrown over their shoulders, they arrived ready for business and knocked on every door in the tier. With nobody home, they enthusiastically broke down four doors, shut down the water to the building, and discovered a break in the pressurized water line that was attached to the hot water heater on the fourth floor. No doubt every unit in the building had the same make and model HW heater.

Ours was a disaster waiting to happen, again and again and again. But still, no response from building management.

As the sun came up, we grabbed coffee across the street and enjoyed the adrenaline rush of having done good work—exactly what we'd set out to do from the start. And we knew the unit owners were grateful we could solve the problem for the property and the residents. They shared our values and understood that, by taking care of the tenants, we were also taking care of their investment. The two are not mutually exclusive, though, and in a perfect world, housing and occupants should take care of one other.

Jim and I could have met those residents with a different set of services if we'd really planned ahead—perhaps creating custom unit guides and laminated on-site tools or providing monthly in-person walkthroughs and coupons to local restaurants. Imagine the effort, time, and missed opportunities spent on any one of these efforts, none of which would likely improve the resident experience. Would tenants pay more? Nope. Would they be more impressed with the company? That's a solid maybe. Would those polished touches help when an entire tier in the building is flooding into your resident's unit? Definitely not. If maybe is the best bet in the scenarios above, why go all-in on maybe? We wanted a sure thing, and it's easier to find that when you work more incrementally, without trying to skip to the end. It freed up the resources of our time, ingenuity, and interests, so we could test other ideas, like a partnership with Kimpton Hotels for emergency stays or a relationship with a great remediation company for floods.

We don't know what investments to make until we test and challenge assumptions. With pointed data and clarity from those tests, you can go farther with less. And that's my specialty.

MANAGE RISK

Most people think entrepreneurs/founders are risk takers. When I tell people I'm quite risk-averse, they assume I'm joking. In fact, everything about my entrepreneurial life has been about creating security, and the property management industry, as I shared earlier, offers an abundance of security. Passive recurring income through monthly management fees, simplicity in fee structures, low startup costs, moderate infrastructure needs, and being an essential business all provide a level of security. Even better, it's an industry where we know what we are up against when it comes to our competition. Many people in the industry do because almost everyone has had a relationship (or many) with a landlord, and most aren't keepers. Property management is an industry seeking a solution, and that's a low-risk proposition. No wonder I fell in love.

Startup methodologies often are conflated with high risk-enterprises, but the startup mindset doesn't need to come at the expense of personal security, ever. In fact, a startup should be designed to reduce overall risk, if designed correctly.

During a blissful pandemic pause in the summer of 2021, Flock was in heavy talks with a potential partner about building a national service-based brand in the home management space. Risk was top-of-mind when we decided to seriously explore a joint-venture. Moving toward a national brand, let alone a partnership, is squarely outside of my comfort zone. The days of having nothing to lose are very much over for us. But being open to change and taking risks are not one and the same.

As I write this, I can't tell you how the partnership and enterprise will turn out. (Perhaps if I find a receptive audience for this work, you will let me know at a reading you attend.) It feels promising, though, because their team is justice-oriented and thoughtful about the role of business to self-elect and advance change. If we know our business can deliver justice, stellar service, and profits at once, we don't want to keep that to ourselves. The partnership seems right because we agreed in those initial conversations that "as entrepreneurs, we're doing all we can to reduce risk in our businesses and lives." With that, we had a shared understanding that risk can be antithetical to creating security. Success in justice-based business is finding an equilibrium, taking measured risks to create more security for ourselves and for the people and places around us as. The profit will follow. Not the other way around. Security might mean a four-day work week, a 401k, a flexible work schedule, or a salary that makes homeownership a given, not an exception in this market and moment.

Home management certainly isn't without risk. But there is so much demand, we believe that risk is measurably lower than it might be in other industries. Managing homes continues to be an essential service we're proud to deliver to an expanding and evolving market, including the homeowners who would love to avail themselves of the ease of leasing with the economic advantages of owning.

HAVING RESILIENCE

We felt invisible at certain stages of our startup journey. Resilience, patience, persistence, and a passion for justice and solving some of the world's biggest problems can be lonely, but it's what led to the successful launch of Impossible Foods. Patrick Brown was a biochemistry professor at Stanford when he self-elected to solve a global problem.[24] Meat consumption is one of our biggest environmental and health challenges, yet we can't seem to shift our appetite. The problem is a critical one to solve. Our reliance on animal-based protein and the damage animal agriculture causes our planet is dangerous to our present and potentially devastating for our future. The problem was so pressing to him that he took an 18-month sabbatical from his cushy ivory tower job to investigate real-life solutions. He is a big thinker who could also think small—so small, in fact, that he found the tiny molecule that makes meat smell and taste like meat. Excited about his findings, he held an academic conference to bring together other great thinkers who could build on his discovery and save human-ity from high cholesterol and greenhouse gas emitting-cow methane. Unfortunately, his colleagues were not as excited,

---

[24] Wikipedia, "Patrick O. Brown."

and the conference fell flat, producing no meaningful results. This is where resilience saved the day.

Patrick knew he was on to something, so he didn't give up. He figured the best way to make an impact wasn't through academia or government grants. The way he would create the biggest change was to compete in the market with his fake meat invention. In 2016 Impossible Burger was born. Three years later, his plant-based meat alternative burger was selling out in Burger Kings across the country. Impossible Burgers have more protein than their meaty counterparts, and their production generates 87% less greenhouse gas and uses 95% less land and 74% less water than beef patties.[25] And guess what? The company is profitable.

When we think of food production, an industrial meat-packing plant might come to mind, but Impossible Burger runs like a tech startup in Silicon Valley. The offices are open, and everyone sits in the same room to increase collaboration and to enjoy company-provided vegan lunches. Patrick is now the CEO, and leads a staff of 750 employees. He says kindness is the top quality he looks for in new team members. You don't have to be vegan to work there, but you do need to be enjoyable to be around. Living their values and stepping up to solve a seemingly impossible challenge is paying off in big ways for Impossible Burger. As they prepare to take the company public, it's currently valued between $4–$10 billion.[26]

---

[25] Wikipedia, "Patrick O. Brown."
[26] Wikipedia, "Patrick O. Brown."

Flock has found that persistence is a professional super power. That and patience. Both were certainly important for us and still are. It took Apple over 20 years to become a success. Netflix didn't turn a profit for six years after launching. Can we imagine a world today without either brand? Indeed, both companies' persistence and drive gave them the momentum to meet a marketplace need, leading both to places in the global communications and entertainment environments respectively. They had to have been resilient AF to get where they are today as business super powers.

We knew our own company had meat on the bones, and we were hungry for business. So we persisted, connected, and went all-in, lining up one conversation after another. Finally, one of our meetings penciled out. We had taken an ad out in Prince of Petworth, a now-iconic DC blog where it seems half of DC spends their free time working to outsmart each other in the comments section. The blog didn't yet have much of an advertiser base, so we could afford to be early adopters and spend some money gaining visibility there. Patrick Blake, a lawyer who'd moved from Atlanta when the recession wreaked havoc on the legal field, saw that Nest ad ten years ago. Like us, he was hustling and building connections, living billable hour to billable hour as all good billable attorneys do. Patrick took us to lunch at an overpriced wine-bar on Connecticut Ave. This restaurant wouldn't let you enjoy happy hour prices at the tables, so we crowded around the bar where Patrick told us he had a client who had just picked up a multi-family property around H Street NE, a newly hot, rapidly developing neighborhood. His client needed a management company. "Happy to help," we said. "We're the best in the city."

Soon thereafter, Fred Hill, who owned that property, scheduled a time to meet. He was barely through the door of our "subleased" offices in a very inconvenient part of town when he gushed over the spaces, commenting on everything from the colors to the office dogs. Without spending any time in sales mode, he said within a handful of minutes sitting across from me, "I gotta tell ya... I'm just gonna tell ya that you're hired. This is gonna be great!" His smile was both convincing and intoxicating. For me, it was as if the seas had parted. I couldn't believe a seven-unit building was in spitting distance.

I'm not sure what kind of investment property I was expecting when we pulled up a week or so later to visit the space. I was likely imagining the homes I managed over the years, all of which enjoyed pride of ownership, even as rentals. This center hall foursquare on a north-south street was probably at one time a grand single family home on a lot of its very own. Unlike neighboring units, this property was unattached—a rarity. The size and scale delivered on my expectations. Everything else was less than impressive, and calling it run-down would be fair. We made our way up the narrow, carpeted, and windowless common stairway and toggled in and out of the units—all of which were in various states of disrepair. A mouse jumped out of a cabinet as we examined one of the kitchens. The whole place needed an energy upgrade—and not the electrical kind, the vibe kind. After we toured the unfinished, moldy basement, Jim and I reconvened over coffee, deeply worried we'd made the wrong play. This building was not at all aligned with the portfolio we wanted to represent, but in our enthusiasm for a big win, we didn't do our due diligence and signed a contract, sight unseen. We underpriced our services and promised far more than we could confidently deliver. But we would persist. We had a hypothesis to test.

Fred and his wife, Christine, turned out to be ideal partners. They gave us carte blanche to improve on that property. Their commitment to creating exceptional spaces for their residents and their enthusiasm for the process has made them, to date, one of the best and most aligned clients we've ever worked with. We still count Fred and Christine as close friends, and their influence and connections have been immeasurably fruitful over the years. Patrick Blake is now Chief Legal Counsel for an international construction company in NYC, and we not only stay in touch, but he continues to offer references and send leads our way. It's almost unimaginable that a tiny little cheap, targeted advertisement in a local blog could be such a game changer. It highlights how valuable every move you make in business can be—even if the move takes a decade to pay off.

As I drafted the story above, Fred Hill called my cell phone. He was locked out of his own house. Within two minutes he had a solution to his problem, and I had proof that I could still cheerfully solve problems and offer a critical service to a growing client base. This is the best-in-class, differentiated service that lets us soar, all while delivering justice. I tapped a senior vice president after Fred pinged me. She runs point on our maintenance division, and I know she's just as invested in delivering the best-in-class service as I am. She got back to me in seconds. How do you create that kind of buy-in from a team from top down, bottom up, and side to side? You trust people, and you give them power (and opportunity, as I'll discuss later).

At every meeting we took over all those years, we promised excellence—something different in a field that delivered disappointment. We weren't just selling a service, we were selling ourselves. We wanted to inspire confidence, build trust, and engage people in our values-based business. Every early partner we had took a leap of faith. They were buying a promise, and promises are meant to be kept.

TRUSTING THE TALENT

Startups, by design, use trust as currency. Without trust, you can't give your teams and talent the power and agency they need to deliver on the work, to innovate, and to make hard decisions in the best interest of the company. The business case for trust and empowerment is compelling. In a 2017 article in *The Harvard Business Review*, Paul Zak published his neuroresearch results on trust in the workplace. "Through his research on the brain chemical oxytocin—shown to facilitate collaboration and teamwork—Zak has developed a framework for creating a culture of trust and building a happier, more loyal, and more productive workforce." His data shows that, "Compared with people at low-trust companies, people at high-trust companies report: 74% less stress, 106% more energy at work, 50% higher productivity, 13% fewer sick days, 76% more engagement, 29% more satisfaction with their lives, 40% less burnout."[27] Talent empowered with trust and agency covers for colleagues and fills gaps. They make decisions in the best interest of the company and, in our case, the mission. They look for efficiency and better, more stream-lined pathways to growth. A trusted team innovates because they are invited to contribute creatively and without fear of micromanagement or lack of support.

Let's talk about this from a justice perspective. If you're burning your teams out by overworking them, micromanaging them, or second guessing them, how can they feel valued and cared for, not just as assets but as people? We have to honor and embrace our talent. They are essential to our success as a business and to our ability to advance justice. If we can't positively impact our team, what business do we have claiming to do it for the community? When people don't trust us, the same is true. When teams can't establish or trust our intention, they won't have a good experience. You trust your talent and hope they trust you and your company. It's a partnership.

Mutual trust was what Toyota taught General Motors after it was forced to close one of its plants in 1982 because of a myriad of production and financial problems. In his book,

---

[27]Zak, "The Neuroscience of Trust, Management Behaviors That Foster Employee Engagement."

The Power of Habit: Why We Do What We Do in Life and Business, Charles Duhigg profiles the car industry and, specifically, the differences between Detroit and Japan. In many ways, it was trust that defined that deep divide. The US auto industry was rusting out, and Detroit factories, once the booming darling of American manufacturing, were running out of gas. No longer a source of coveted jobs, the city's factories had begun delivering a mediocre product that couldn't compete in its own marketplace against the Japanese carmakers that started to dominate the roads. Japanese cars were becoming ever-present for good reason: They were more reliable, cheaper, and more efficient.

Toyota wanted to increase their market in the US, and GM needed to learn the famed "Toyota Production System" that consistently produced quality cars at a lower cost. So Toyota and GM formed a partnership to reopen the US carmaker's doomed plant using "The Toyota Way" principles the company had perfected over decades of car manufacturing in Japan. At the core of Toyota's lean manufacturing magic was decentralized decision making, where assembly line workers were given the responsibility and authority to take immediate action to fix the problem, even if it meant "pulling the cord" to shut down production, an action that could cost car manufacturers $15,000 a minute.[28] In other words, Toyota *trusted* their workers.

The hallmark of any auto manufacturing workflow is the assembly line. At each station, a team member is responsible

---

[28] Duhigg, *The Power of Habit.*

for their part in building the vehicle. It might be installing a panel or hood or other component. The Detroit model insists that the line keeps moving to maintain production schedules and reduce losses. The problem is that the line leaves no room for quality control until it is too late. If a screw doesn't connect properly or falls behind the door panel unattached, there is nothing to be done because there is no stopping the line. But as that new car buyer rattles around with a loose screw in their driver's side door, you can bet GM won't be counting them as a customer for life. The Toyota model takes the opposite approach. If the quality of the vehicle is diminished as a result of rushing the production process, the loss becomes cumulative and leads to an inferior and inconsistent product. That waters down the brand value, reducing profits and market position. Instead, Toyota encourages stopping the line. Every worker, no matter their role, is empowered to pull the cord, stop the line, study the problem, and resolve the issue. Only then does the line continue. Management serves the assembly line work rather than simply supporting it. They step up to assist the team member with whatever they need to clear the problem or resolve the complexity. Each team member contributes to real-time quality control. Managers trust their talent, and their talent consistently builds a car that performs better in every category—safety, design, style, and cost. Short term "losses" are actually investments offering opportunities to refine processes and products and to learn from those building the product or delivering the service.

When GM reopened their plant two years later, the rehired union auto workers were hesitant to "stop the line" as they were used to marking an error in production with a Post-it note and hoping it got fixed by a colleague further down the line. But as managers and assembly line work-ers learned to trust each other, they found that the system worked. By 1986, production in the reopened plant doubled and absenteeism plummeted.[29]

Trust in business (and life) isn't always easy. But in business, distrust becomes quite expensive because double-check-ing and/or doubting the decision making, work product, and ideas of the team you pay to do good work is ineffective. It bogs down organizations and significantly limits growth pos-sibilities because if you're going backward to double-check all day, you certainly aren't going forward.

For better or worse, I tend to err on the side of being too trusting and, for the most part, assume good intentions from team members. Still, there are some aspects of the com-pany I'm overly attached to and protective of. I'm particularly inflexible when it comes to branding and identity because, well, it's our company's signature and a labor of love. "Hands off, please." That was the culture I cultivated. But at some point, it wasn't a good look.

When you have something to sell without a real track record and service is your business, you're essentially sell-ing your brand identity. Jim and I took that very seriously.

---

[29] Duhigg, *The Power of Habit*.

We knew we would stand out and set a new bar if we were intentional and deliberate about the way we presented ourselves and talked about ourselves, our services, and our mission. This is how we would create the connection between community and corporation. Our entire value system needed to be reflected in the branding for the company. We had to be accessible but exclusive, trendy, intriguing, attractive, and deeply committed to the community. Our branding has always been not just a reflection of the company but of me as well. It's hyper-personal.

Nobody would disagree that our branding is on point. From the name to the visual identity, we stood out from the start. Our approach was intriguing, intimate, and honest. We were telling a story, nesting ourselves, and settling into a business that we knew could create change. Who doesn't love nesting? Landing on the name was almost instant. And no nest is complete without a bird. I'm a big bird lover. It started during those Colorado summers I would spend on my grandparent's farm. I trailed after Grandma Sue as she tended to the needs of her flock of sheep. Like her, I marveled at the majestic nature of the hawks, eagles, falcons, and herons that hovered over us while "we" worked. When she could take the time to do so, she made her way to her art studio. That space was awash in light, with bright white walls, high ceilings, and a watercolor-stained desk that seemed to be sized to fit the oval office. There, perched on her stool, brush in hand, Grandma Sue's gorgeous birds would take flight on her canvas.

Since Jim and I met in Tucson, we settled on the desert quail to represent our brand. Our orange bird was striking, and immediately, folks took notice. Everything about our brand set us apart, so I was particularly stubborn when it came to modifying anything about it. The website was a particular point of pride and a hell of a deliverable given that we didn't have any clue how to write, build, maintain, or market one. I met with someone recently who said, "I only paid $10,000 for my branding."

"Really?" I responded.

"Yes, ten different times."

That's how we felt about our website journey. There was a lot of trial and error, much of which stemmed from us trying to save money. Running a lean company is key, but not when doing so leads to a waste of time and money.

Eventually, we nailed the site, and the talent we needed was already on staff. Mark was someone I hired back in my non-profit days. He was swept into the Nest family when he did side jobs taking pictures of spaces, producing promotional videos, or guiding us on our digital footprint. We grew up with Mark as he did with us, and he's been in a part-time role since the very beginning. Today, Mark works as an award winning, highly skilled videographer and web developer for us and many others. We have Mark to thank for our exquisite digital footprint and branding.

Mark didn't just Nest, he **was** Nest. He still is. That was a game changer. Having someone work on brand and identity is much harder with third party consultants—and consequently much slower and more expensive. Mark was able to put together the most stylish and practical site in the industry at the time. The site wasn't just used to sell our services; we also used it to showcase our spaces. Listings were prominently featured, and we received feedback that ours was the site people came to when looking for the best rentals in the District. But over time, as with all things digital, websites (even among our industry) started to look polished. The management software we worked with offered an out-of-the-box, slightly customizable site that married the listings to the software. The "best in industry," custom site Mark built for us required a lot of custom attention. We were constantly tending to details around our growing number of listings—changing availability dates, updating prices, adding new images to the listings. But our flagship and most profitable brand still stood out among the competition. This was an intentional part of our business model. I will do a deep dive into the value of differentiation later, but for now, it's fair to say that being different with the increasingly onerous back-end of our website was for the birds. It took me a minute to get there, though.

Grace is the president of Flock. As I write this, she's a few months shy of a ten year anniversary, which she'll be celebrating with her newborn son, our newest Flockster. Grace started as a leasing specialist and today largely runs every aspect of the company that's not geared toward external affairs, the brand, business development, and the incubation of new birds. Grace approached me about an out-of-the-box website transition because the time and energy required to keep the Nest site updated was too significant. "Never," I said. "Case closed." Later, I was talked into attending a demo, so I could see with my own two, wise eyes how "on-brand" this new site would be with the opportunity to customize.

I took the meeting. I was unimpressed. The customization we wanted was off the table, and that was a non-starter for me. But as Grace shared more data around how much time and money this transition would save, I could no longer make a business case for spending a full-time-employee equivalent every year just so my dreams of being different could be actualized. Surely, there was a better investment that would work out more favorably.

The decision took two weeks from idea presentation to my full sign-off. The Nest website today is, well, just fine. What it isn't is an incredible resource vacuum. Property listings in our management software are sent to all the marketing sites with the push of a button. The integration is elegant and foolproof. There are no delays in marketing, inconsistent listings, or errors in pricing or availability. The team doesn't have to manage content over multiple platforms separately. They instead have more time to engage with the client, deliver stellar service, and respond to problems that need solutions in real time, not when they have time.

Our old website was failing us, and as long as I insisted we keep it, I was, too. There was, however, a business case for using that transition to reconsider our branding across the family of companies. While Nest is important as our legacy brand, it's not the only business we were running. The Flock DC identity was, in fact, the mother bird that needed greater visibility and broader wings. So, we rebuilt Flock's digital identity. As long as Nest was acting like our biggest bird, Flock would be a side-bar. Keeping things same-same would actually limit growth potential, mute profitability, and stop us from advancing our social justice values. Had I lacked trust in Grace's ability to see a better path, I would have left the chance to innovate and expand our reach and visibility on the table. My creativity wouldn't have been triggered. Instead, we used that opportunity to invest in our family of birds, so each could fly higher than ever—particularly when it comes to justice investments. Today, Flock's digital identity and recognizability has only grown because we availed ourselves of the simplicity in using the out-of-the-box tool for a single business unit. The brand refresh was perfectly timed.

When we began our digital renovation, we were also launching our housing justice initiative, birdSEED. This philanthropic endeavor offers no-strings, down payment grants to first time home buyers in our region who are Black, Indigenous, People of Color. Seeds need water, but they don't want to be watered down. Flock's brand investment helped others understand how birdSEED fit naturally into our ethos as a company. I had to release my grip on certain aspects of the business because they outgrew my homegrown, gritty skillset and, in some cases, (though hardest to admit) my vision. There are certain things we need to let go of, and the sooner the better when those things are essentially holding us back. I had to let go to fly high.

RUN LEAN, GO WITH IT, OR LET IT GO

I wonder how long it took the Lyft team to shave the signature bright pink mustache that adorned their driver's front grill when the company first drove onto the scene and worked to differentiate their car sharing service from dominant Uber. It's not easy letting go. I'm sure someone was really sad to see that 'stache in the rear view.

If, at the start, we had tasked ourselves with building out a company that could accommodate a thousand plus units at a time, surely, we would have failed. For those among us lamenting the built-in speakers we have in our ceiling, there is a lot to be said for not going all-in on something until you see how the environment, the market, the economy, and, in our case, the community will change. It's very likely we wouldn't have been able to deliver a scalable property management company that could service 5,500 residents successfully. That's in large part due to our heavy reliance on talent. We deployed a servant leadership model that paired with our differentiation and social justice values. But if those experiments and approaches had not been penciled-out, it's likely we would be burning out our staff like the balance of the industry, falling victim to the complexity and relentless volume of work property management requires. We could be top of the heap as the best of the worst, with a revolving door of unhappy, used, and abused team members. It's a brutal industry, and a natural us vs. them combat stance emerges when there isn't alignment on what problems need solving or resources allocated to solve them. Tenants can and should have reasonably high expectations for their space. Investors, using a metrics-based (read: bottom-line driven) approach to tracking their real estate's performance, are inclined to suppress expenses. This paradigm delivers a loser in almost every situation if the lens is purely focused on short-term profit. That model didn't work for us. What has worked is iterative and evolves as our residents, clients, community, and staff needs change.

Whether it's a website, a staff member, or an entire business unit, you have to be willing to cut and run if it's not working. Because if it's not working *for* you, it's working *against* you and the company. Being operationally nimble and lean is not just for the startup stage; it's an applicable principle you can incorporate into your company for the long haul. Eric Reis, the business influencer I referenced earlier, presents a formula for testing vs. building. It centers on conducting market research while creating prototypes and testing theories. Rather than build the whole development, start with the model home. Or better yet, just design a sweet brochure with sample layouts and start talking to potential home buyers.

In his book, *The Lean Startup*, Reis offers a compelling story about a basic, unmet need that was observed in India where less than seven percent of the population had laundry in their homes. "People either did their wash by hand or paid a Dhobi to take their dirty laundry to a nearby river to wash and return, perhaps a bit cleaner, many days later." It's fair to say, this was a problem worth solving. But producing a comprehensive plan to serve even portions of India with better, more timely laundry service was a complex, resource-intensive proposition with virtually unlimited pathways to success or failure. The opportunity costs associated with a "build it and they will come" approach isn't necessary when a lean startup model which encourages experimentation and prototyping can be used, allowing the testing of designs before building them out. Akshay Mehra had a hypothesis that there was a possible solution to the lack of options for laundry in India. Akshay had been part of the Tide and Pantene brands and "thought he could make laundry services available to people who previously could not afford them" (67). He "joined Village Laundry Services (VLS)... and began a series of experiments to test its business assumptions." (67) "In 2008, Village Laundry Service mounted a consumer-grade laundry machine on the back of a pickup truck parked on a street in Bangalore. The experiment cost less than $8,000 and had the simple goal of proving that people would hand over their laundry and pay to have it cleaned." (67) It worked. From there, they could design and scale a laundry service that met the consumer's key needs: convenience, speed, and proximity. In less than a year, Village Laundry Service grew from three laundry kiosks to 20 in Bangalore and Mumbai.[30] They tested a model and it worked.

Focusing on small, low-cost concepts or products makes it possible to assess viability instead of investing in and building tools, services, or products that customers or partners may not want or need. Prototypes might even attract the wrong customer altogether. It's far better to find out what doesn't work—and what does—as quickly as possible.

The testing model might be as simple as a product add-on or premium service to a small percentage of an existing

---

[30]Ries, *The Lean Startup: How Today's Entrepreneurs Use Continuous Innovation to Create Radically Successful Businesses*, 67.

client base. Once we had enough clients, we could test services/products within our own business ecosystem. We decided to test preventive maintenance as an add-on service. In management, this is one of the hardest services to deliver with reliability and regularity. The proptech solutions were poorly designed and failed to provide an interface that was customized to workflows and client friendly. They lacked sophisticated tools for recurring activities, and we believed we could deliver a better service and increase profits if we had a preventive maintenance program that serviced the entire portfolio. This included draining hot water heaters, inspecting sump pumps, replacing back up batteries, swapping out old plumbing supply lines that could easily fail and lead to flooding, caulking windows, and replacing hose bibs with all-weather materials. Thinking through the logistical gymnastics it would take to service something that wasn't broken, thousands of times over a short period, was dizzying. So we started small, offering a discreet segment of our single family home portfolio three preventive maintenance services that owners could opt in to via a simple form. Of the 50 units we sampled, about half enthusiastically opted for two or more. Each of the three services were water related (water = threat). This meant we could send the same technician for all three tasks. We also had an in-house master plumbing technician, so we could leverage in-house talent, plus vendors, to meet high-volume tickets in a short period of time. Scheduling 25 tickets was a much more manageable proposition than 1,000+ unit owners opting for a host of preventive maintenance services that required multiple vendors. Could we get to serving 1,000+ unit owners? Absolutely. Could we get there without testing (v. taxing) our work flows, pricing, and service standards? Nope. In this scenario, we set the bar. There was no reason to set ourselves up for failure when what we really wanted to deliver was a win for all our stakeholders. The slow play, low investment sampling of the service helped us scale.

We're now able to deliver preventive maintenance in various categories that owners opt in to in perpetuity to streamline communications and book work with quarterly lead time. We have room to improve on and expand this work, but we won't do it at the expense of delivering a best in class core management experience for our residents and our clients, whose investment property we are trusted to manage. That doesn't mean we can't get creative as we grow—something we particularly had to do when we avoided taking outside investments.

We needed to be lean and scrappy when we launched Nest. I wasn't interested in taking on debt, so Nest had to generate revenue from the start, and we decided to get dollars in the door with services that could generate cash today but still, more or less, complement our core management business. We called it our three-legged bird and offered property management, design and light renovation, and what we believe would be our most innovative bird leg—relocation services. Painting miles upon miles of baseboards and installing flooring and chandeliers did make it rain a bit, just enough to cover our small financial outlay to operate. And we knew the management contracts would start to multiply. But our most innovative service, relocation, emerged as our most attractive potential revenue stream. Plus, we could teach team members to do it easily, unlike plumbing.

What do I mean by relocation? We matched prospective renters with the perfect rental. We started to notice, as we shopped our property management services around town, that we were hearing more and more stories describing frustration in finding their perfect nest, particularly when they were trying to pull off a long-distance move. From my perspective, the business case for solving this problem in the market was substantial (if largely based on happy hour anecdotes, which can still generate valid hypotheses).

Real estate agents (for the most part) didn't offer a relocation service for renters, and outside of corporate relocation specialists, nobody was available to smooth out this process for tenants searching for units from afar. Further, we were looking to take the hassle out of home management and attract property owners/investors (accidental landlords) who were burned out or just plain bad at managing their own apartments or single family homes. At that time, people found rentals by combing Craigslist or apartments.com, and most of those listings featured a handful of badly-lit and poorly-composed photos of a space. The ads often violated fair housing laws, though likely unintentionally. Transacting long distance is a flat-out hassle. Corresponding with nine to five leasing agents at large-format buildings can be challenging from a different time zone, and coordinating with out-of-towners was tough for the one-off landlords, too. Most of those owners are tied to their day jobs. All of these factors make looking for housing long distance an almost impossible proposition. This was a serious opportunity for us to market our services while making money and increasing visibility in the marketplace. In a perfect world, the relocation client would become a tenant in a new property we would begin to manage. The problem: There is no perfect world in relocation.

We set about creating a simple service. We offered industry and neighborhood expertise and sold that as value added to our clients in need of housing from afar. We would look at listings in the area that met their criteria, take quick videos of the spaces, and give them highly-customized insider info on the best spaces and places in the city. Clients would pay a flat fee, and we would handle all of the logistics. After a phone intake, we did daily searches (on Craigslist) and decided which listings to tour. We estimated this entire engagement to take no more than six total hours before we found the ideal spot for them.

As it turned out, our relocation services brought out the worst in everyone. We offered little structure and set vague expectations for our client base. On the other hand, our clients wanted first-class seating on a budget airline. They thought we had a secret list of deeply affordable, yet perfectly-situated and -appointed spaces all over the city. With parking, too! They also expected we were available, without restriction, all of the time to help them with their hunt. We sent one walkthrough video after another only to get a "we're disappointed" reply, with a laundry list of dislikes about every space we introduced them to.

We were essentially doing asynchronous virtual showing because this was before Facetime and there was no real-time visual way to engage with our clients while we were in the unit. So only the day after we sent a video would we hear that the client wanted more detail on the depth of a closet and hoped we might negotiate, on their behalf, a discount in the leasing fee and parking, of course. And if we could check on whether that block had a big mosquito problem, that would be great, too. Fun fact: A surprising number of people will view a bedroom, in person or virtually, look at the closet, survey the room again, and then ask if there is *another* closet—when very clearly there is not. Perhaps it's next to the non-existent parking space. It never hurts to ask?

Relocation was the worst/best business decision I ever made. Like a few other businesses I launched over the years, we were pulling in about five dollars per hour. I would have been better off repainting units and fixing the toilet chains. We had to let it go. Relocation was a fail, no matter how brilliant it was on paper. We may have been solving a problem for a client, but that was their problem. It couldn't be ours. We had to focus on what we did best: manage homes, not locate them. How we refined and fine-tuned that service became essential to the growth we would experience over the decade.

When I talk about letting go, I'm not just talking about letting go of crappy business ideas. I'm talking about firing clients, too. No matter how much they pay, at some point you realize it's not worth the pain and suffering. This is especially true in a high-touch service environment. The lesson? When things *only* look good on paper, head to the shredder.

SURROUND YOURSELF WITH PEOPLE WHO CARE ABOUT YOUR COMPANY'S FUTURE, NOT JUST THEIR OWN

Early in business, it's hard to know if the people you've surrounded yourself with have the same enthusiasm for the work and the mission. It's easy to assume they do because generous compensation for early team members is often set aside for a promising future. But there are many vendors and consultants who will slip through your ecosystems who don't believe in what you're doing and, instead, see you and your company in terms of billable hours. It's hard to develop trust when you aren't sure what you need from a paid advisor, but the exposure to the company is substantial when you trust the wrong provider, partner, or vendor.

Ironically, the biggest threat to our businesses was the lawyer we hired to help set up a number of our interrelated entities. Roy was a referral introduced as someone who specialized in helping prepare the governing and incorporation documents for employee-owned entities. "It's easy," he said. "I do this all the time," he assured us. He let us know what the work would likely entail and the anticipated cost; then, he set about structuring our operating agreements, valuation formulas, and shareholder documents. We had calls about our vision for valuation. And I was particularly passionate and inexperienced all at once when it came to the valuation model. So, why not go for gold. (I'm so embarrassed to say I was certain a 1.2x trailing 12 months earnings made sense. For the layperson reading this, I was bold enough to think the business—with no real track record—would be worth a year or 1.2x a year of our earnings. This was for Roost, our employee-owned enterprise I'll brag about later.) Giving away part of my company to the people who helped build it was a career-changing professional decision.

No matter how optimistic and trusting I was, the operating agreement and organizational structure designed by this attorney should have been illegal. (Given that we were paying market-rate hourly fees and eating up more hours than we could really afford, the entire enterprise should have been illegal.) The corporate structure for Roost was incompatible with tax law, the agreement did nothing to protect the company, and the valuation model was so unrealistic, it created a massive financial exposure. This last detail became evident when we suffered mightily during the first employee-owner exit. A key team member, who never satisfied full payment of her shares, was, due to the way the promissory notes were structured, owed a huge payout that put our employee-owned company in a precarious financial position for years as we recovered from the loss. This was the ultimate cost of using an advisor who did not care about the future of the company. We brought counsel in-house to control not only cost, but culture and pride of work. Plus, we did it creatively and in alignment with our company values.

Pavan, a fellow parent at my son's school, became a close friend over the years. As in-house counsel at a large government contracting firm, he was in a constant state of harried existence. Suffering a two-hour, round-trip commute, he was resigned to missing anything that wasn't scheduled well in advance and adjusting for the total lack of flexibility his work offered. Pavan was breathless picking up kids and rushing when dropping them off. His work was somewhere in the middle, and his professional and personal joy were nowhere in sight. We talked often about his sacrifice as we wondered aloud what more there was to give up for an employer that seemed disinterested in giving up much for him. His request for a single work-from-home day was denied. We chatted while our sons discovered their mutual dislike of basketball. He shared the dream of having his own practice. Breaking the math down, he would make the same salary working a third of the hours if he could pull together enough clients for his own practice. The familial and financial wins available were hard to argue with, but building a book of business is tough and takes a lot of time—especially in DC, where lawyers are the second state bird, right behind real estate agents.

As our relationship developed, Pavan became an invaluable thought partner as I struggled to navigate our poorly executed corporate structure. He's both justice-driven and entrepreneurial, and we had a clear alignment in our value systems and our agreement that the Flock business model is a critical counterpoint to business as usual. Eventually, it became clear we were the answers to each other's problems. I needed in-house counsel I could trust, but I couldn't afford or justify it full-time. Pavan needed an anchor "client" that offered enough security to risk hanging his own shingle. Today, Pavan is the fractional in-house counsel for our Flock family of companies. His growing list of clients benefit from his ability to choose to work on what matters to him most, and, like his work with Flock, he has self-elected to use a social justice lens to deliver exceptional, accessible legal counsel.

When I look back on the collision course my former attorney put us on, I think, I should have known better. But as a self-taught business owner, I hired him precisely because I didn't know what I didn't know. And we didn't have cash for a second opinion. The Hippocratic Oath and the rules of bar admission aren't quite the same because plenty of harm was done to our business when an attorney prioritized profit over sound representation. I had no remedy for this abysmal advisor, except to warn off other early-stage, green entrepreneurs who sought referrals for strong legal counsel on business matters. Regardless, as a lean startup, when the risk Roy exposed us to revealed itself, it was with little hesitation that we fired his ass.

OPTIMIZE OPERATIONS

Operating in an industry with an abysmal reputation makes the delivery of superior service that much more attainable. But remember, best in class can't, in practice, be "best of the worst." Delayed replies to resident needs isn't much better than not replying at all. A minimally maintained home may not be much better than one that's shabby and poorly maintained.

We intended from the start to set entirely new standards for performance. We invited our clients, residents, and even vendors to expect more of us and fret less over whether they would get service or respect when needed. But outpacing competition wasn't just about having a startup ethos and our differences. It was about delivery and an exceptional living experience with sophisticated systems and processes. This was a taller order than I thought in a business that is complex and has slim margins and bullies that make the work that much more challenging.

But the industry creates opportunities to deliver an essential service that's only improved upon when aligned with a social justice values system. At Flock, we provide people with homes—dignified, safe, well-maintained, high-quality spaces to call their own, if only for a lease term. That responsibility is an honor, a privilege, and a matter of justice. As managers of homes, we are able to have an immeasurable impact on people's quality of life. Being responsive, empathic, kind, and caring are core values and drive our best-in-class service. We choose to put profits last (but not least) in favor of building a business model that is just and purposeful. Cared-for places and spaces along with happy residents, staff, and clients lead to more robust, joyful, and stable communities. This sounds great on paper and in the core values section of the website, but unless you can operationalize the work, you're telling stories out of turn.

Just like Steve Blank defines the startup in terms of scale, we decided early on we wanted to build an enterprise that could grow and have impact at once. We went from managing a handful of properties to tending to thousands of residents at one time. Each one, on any given day, may be moving in, moving out, experiencing a heating or cooling problem, needing a new roommate, wanting to get rid of a roommate, adopting a pet (or hiding one), making too much noise, complaining about noise, smoking weed, complaining about weed smoke, unable to make rent, or wanting a copy of their lease (urgently) because they are at the DMV right this minute. Some will call the emergency line when they see a roach or email urgently because the leaves in the alley are piling up and getting moldy, which is bad for allergies. They will ask for a new garbage can because theirs was stolen. This is just a sampling of all the problems we work to solve cheerfully throughout the day for our residents. For the owners of the units occupied by those 5,500 residents, we're tracking industry regulations, collecting rent, inspecting the unit, managing maintenance and emergency requests, and making sure they have proper licenses and tax filings. Without a nimble, client-forward approach to the work and a deep interest in refining and improving on systems as they begin to fail under the volume of requests, there is no way to successfully deliver excellence in this particular industry.

It's little wonder most management companies are smaller in scale or failing at a large scale. This isn't a matter of personal opinion: Real-estate investment trusts were bullish on the rental market and saw an opportunity to pad their

portfolio with foreclosed home purchases after the debt crisis left many homebuyers homeless in the late 2000s. Wall
Street analysts and potential shareholders, however, were
skeptical. Maintaining thousands of homes of different sizes,
ages, and conditions across an entire metropolitan area by
one operation seemed like a logistical nightmare. "How can
you operate and create scale in that situation?" Sam Zell, the
billionaire real estate investor, told CNBC in 2013. "I don't
know how anybody can monitor thousands of houses."

But Flock can. And we do it in lean startup mode.

There was a lot of trial and error, but with the core values that guided our vision and our mission, we had a solid
frame of reference when it came to knowing when, why, and
how to improve on our processes. If we weren't serving our
stakeholders well, we needed to make adjustments. We continuously stopped and studied where we were operationally.
And sometimes what we saw was failing us in a big way. Many
of our early policies and procedures were awful. Though we
intended to work in a paperless environment, there were
some things we couldn't do electronically (yet), like managing receipts. Imagine a stack of receipts, none of which had
the information we needed from techs who were in a constant state of runnin' and gunnin.' On a good day, a handful
of receipts had property addresses. Some had been floating around in wallets or cars so long they had faded. Those
were the receipts we actually got back from our field team.
Back at the office, someone was tasked with taping receipts
to scratch paper to be scanned. We stored the paper as a
backup to the soft copy files that we were almost certainly

not organizing properly on our computers/cloud based folders if at all (with the exception of the paper receipt plague that doesn't resolve easily). As an early stage company, you naturally show up where the greatest needs live, and those needs are largely housed in our properties, not in our stack of receipts. Except the problems we were solving were both back of the house and front of the house at that point: no receipt, no reimbursement. We had an operational threat to negotiate and resolve. Pair that problem with our habit of keeping staff on board because they were "nice" and wasting all kinds of time because we were creating workarounds to our own workarounds. We joked our systems were made of joint compound. It looked good, but it was temporary, not structural. Though we were delivering a stellar service, we were leaving money on the table and burning out our systems and good talent. What worked for one portfolio size wouldn't for another. At 20 doors, we changed everything. We did the same at 50 and at 200 and so on and so on. You have to be willing to scrap the whole thing and start over to deliver a better, more agile service that's also financially viable, no matter the cost, even if it's counterintuitive. If whatever you invested to get where you are is no longer paying dividends, move your investment for better performance.

Many years after starting the company, I was at an industry conference. They broke us into those painful working groups to brainstorm ideas about ways to keep our staff happy. One gentleman (who, as a white, male owner in his mid-60s, was truly the industry stereotype) announced with pride that every Friday, he gave the "girls" who did the filing, a five dollar Starbucks gift card. After a long pause, I looked at him and asked, "Why are you filing paper?" It wasn't worth commenting on the balance of his statement. But it's clear that my industry remains bogged down in outdated systems and archaic cultures. Applying the basic principles of operational efficiency by staying open to change and designing workflows that traded on technologies that streamlined our work was one of our very best decisions.

Operations and systems aren't fixed. To function best, they need to be a work in progress. Early on, we were good at leveraging technology to streamline workflows and create better outcomes for both clients and our staff. We understood, or perhaps learned the hard way, that not every process was designed to scale. What fit us perfectly and made us feel like a thousand bucks system-wise could be something we'd grow right out of, looking like an awkward adolescent. In the early days, we used to let this throw us. But then we built room into our business cadence to stop and re-evaluate our approaches. As we grew, which was a natural progression for our company, systems failed. Big time. Rather than letting that derail us, we planned for it. Our staff of professional problem solvers was given agency to probe our patterns and not only recommend changes, but also to make those suggestions a reality if they made us better at our work.

The trick to building scalable, client forward systems that work means being open to change when better pathways to productivity open up. Sometimes the lessons don't come easily. So over time, I developed a mantra: Study the work. If there is a smarter, better, faster way to deliver an exceptional client and staff experience, then do it and don't look back. Even if it means taking a bath on a previous investment. We once used a support tool to manage accounts payable. It was an immediate game changer for us, outsourcing a tedious and time-consuming activity with significant room for human error. The tool offered a technology ecosystem to manage financial transactions with an approval feature for a segment of our clients. It was a win-win, economizing work flows while increasing transparency with customers. We invested an enormous amount of time, money, and energy operationalizing that tool. But a few years went by, and we were beginning to sag beneath the weight of our growth. We studied bottlenecks in our workflows and discovered that the very tool that we adopted to streamline our work was doing the opposite. Vendors' payments were lagging, our reputation as a vendor-friendly company was in jeopardy over stalled payments, and our accounting cadence was faltering. Managing cash with so much money "in transition" was becoming a financial burden and a risk. Some clients were too busy to approve invoices while others had time on their hands and were inclined to deny payments if they didn't care for—or just didn't understand—the service. Our elegant solution to an operational problem had become a giant pain. It not only wasn't meeting our clients' needs, but was in fact creating a client problem.

In almost all cases, we've found that our greatest solutions are temporary. When I reflect on that accounts payable solution, I'm glad we didn't look at that investment of resources as wasted. Continuing to use a system that didn't work anymore would have been far more painful. And growth with tools that don't scale or meet our client-forward ethos ultimately works against us. Furthermore, the longer you work a system that's not working, the longer it takes to back out of it. So just like that, we bailed and discovered that the management software we were already completely bought into had expanded services to support the need this failing third party vendor was supposed to meet. If we can't solve our own problems, how can we cheerfully solve problems for our clients?

Every system investment or innovation should enhance your client and or staff holder experience. At a minimum, one of your stakeholders should benefit positively from your operations. Any part of your operations that doesn't should be eliminated or redesigned—and fast. Staying ahead of the curve operationally relies on a cultural and organizational commitment to innovation. Stay open to and interested in solutions you didn't know you needed. As our portfolio grew, our high touch, empathic communication brand started to struggle under the weight of crushing email correspondence. The best among us couldn't keep up, and response times and follow-through was suffering. Grace, as president, is tasked with seeing problems as they emerge and resolving them with new approaches to the work before we suffer serious missteps. For example, she saw things trending poorly and moved quickly to adopt Slack across our business units. By segmenting communications platforms and moving internal correspondence to Slack, we were able to reserve the email inbox for clients and residents. Plus fans. And the real time interactions Slack afforded us kept us engaged with ease throughout the day. Email no longer bogged us down the same way. And we were very grateful for that move to Slack when the pandemic hit because it was the only way we could create a casual place to convene as a staff virtually.

As we grew, we needed vendors, products, and tools that could grow with us because, at some point, we understood that to get where we were going, we needed everything to scale. We switched banks, changed insurance brokers, and added in-house counsel. We upgraded vehicles and started using management coaches. We expanded our office spaces and started outsourcing tasks that were bogging down staff without adding value to our clients and residents. I don't regret any of it, and I'm also poised for when we battle another adolescent phase, hungry and growing and needing us to be ready to make quick, strategic changes for the better, even if it means cutting losses in some cases.

Fairness and justice set us apart, and we invested in both as we grew the company. We understood early that those values had to be paired with best-in-class services, and we also needed to know how we would slot into the industry. Once we got our wings, we weren't interested in managing a few hundred units—the typical client base of a mom-and-pop shop. Nor were we interested in the scale and shareholder accountability that defined real estate investments. Trusts (REITS) and large-scale investors who bought and managed their own "assets," residents be damned; their job is to create robust returns year after year. That model means the only way to increase cash flow is to raise rent (which is done as often as the law allows) and decrease or postpone services.

This means little maintenance and few investments in improvements of any kind.

And for the big corporate behemoths who do manage thousands of homes at once, they aren't interested so much in delivering quality housing with a great experience to their residents, but instead, they are interested in bigger profits to shareholders. In her *Atlantic* article, "When Wall Street is Your Landlord," Alana Semeuls profiles those management giants, observing that, "With help from the federal government, institutional investors became major players in the rental market. They promised to return profits to their investors and convenience to their tenants. Investors are happy. Tenants are not."[31]

"The investors argued that they could be good landlords—better, in fact, than cash-strapped small-timers," according to Diane Tomb, the executive director of the National Rental Home Council.[32] Established in 2014, the trade group for single-family rental companies "professionalized" a sector traditionally run by mom-and-pop landlords, bringing with them 24/7 responses to maintenance requests and a deep pool of capital they can spend on homes. They also projected they could make money, which no one had done on a large scale in the home-rental business. Clearly, the market revealed a problem that needed solving. Residents needed well-managed housing. But it was also clear that profitability was the primary

---

[31] Semeuls, "When Wall Street is Your Landlord."
[32] Semeuls, "When Wall Street is Your Landlord."

key performance indicator for these large investment firms, and tenants' quality of life was an afterthought at best.

When tenants were top of mind among the REIT's corporate leaders, it was because they were being leveraged to handle repairs and maintenance that should have been handled by the management firm. They leaned on tenants, creating a burden to improve margins by denying maintenance requests or requiring them of the resident. Deposits weren't considered placeholders but rather advance payment for what landlords would find a way to put on a tenant's parting invoice, no matter the statutory acceptability of wear and tear and the resident's entitlement to those dollars. Of course, the cost benefit of fighting wasn't always worth it, especially when fighting a bureaucratic company whose purpose is to relieve you of those funds. Across the board, these commonplace practices among large-format landlords managing their own assets would be considered unethical at best by the balance of the industry. But these practices didn't invent themselves and have been commonplace for as long as we've had rentals, renters, and the slumlord to oversee both. The slumlord in this scenario just has corporate offices.

In the meantime, mom-and-pop shops handle about 200 doors before they cap out. It's just enough to make a decent profit for the owners, provided they keep salaries "fairly" low along with fixed and variable expenses. I remember 200 doors with great fondness. It was a life-defining moment. The profit could be mine. Ours, it could be *ours*. But profit and equity are not one in the same. I was, I am, building a company that is growing in value. It has value and would be attractive to a buyer. At any time, frankly. Flock is an investment that can and will grow in value over time. So unlike other mom-and-pops, I understood real profit was the long (equity) game—not the end of the month or annualized net operating income.

We remain unwilling to see the benefits of reduced labor costs or decreased resident services. We know refining and investing in sophisticated systems and amplifying our effort to deliver a stellar service leads to a more valuable and *valued* company. We stay open to new ways of doing business.

Let's revisit our receipt issue. Certainly, I thought, some techie has figured out this receipt situation, and indeed, someone had. Expensify came into the FinTech space just when we needed them, offering electronic receipt management and expense reporting using smart phones and artificial intelligence. At the same time, our property management software was pushing out new updates, and we were able to remove the barriers techs had in getting (most) receipts back to the office for billing without having to go back to the office. Our full-time, receipt-taping position could be redeployed to work on tasks that added value to our client and resident experience rather than subtracting from it. The day we had the shredding company pick up endless boxes of tape and paper was a good day.

Was a transition to electronic receipts management a light lift? Far from it. The process was disruptive, created a learning curve, and was generally hated by our techs on the front end. But it eventually smoothed out, helped us scale much more easily, and increased reimbursements substantially. We were better able to focus on service deliverables and minimize payroll dedicated to back office tasks that added no value to clients or colleagues. This isn't common in the industry because it's hard as hell to do. Once again, because mediocrity is the mean, there's little to incentivize management company owners to make drastic changes. Yet we believe it makes all the difference, and different is our normal.

PART FOUR

CHAPTER 9

DIFFERENT OUT
OF THE GATE

Our community is aflutter when DC has a snow flurry. In the early hours of a decent storm, you'll find flash snowball fights and folks using trash can lids as sleds in the park. But after a few inches and a few days, the thrill is gone. About six years ago, I was trying to escape a snowstorm that had my little family shut in for over a week. At some point, desperate for a change of scenery, my four year old and I schlepped to the bus and made our way to the Logan Ace Hardware on 14th St. NW. It was one of the few running routes in the city and a straight shot. DC doesn't perform so well in the snow, but Gina's store does well in any kind of weather. We ducked into the storefront, dusted ourselves off, and set about buying balloons because balloons are perfect for any occasion. I knew I would need some support if we wanted to leave with helium-filled balloons, and I dreaded having to track someone down who would show any interest in meeting my needs. But the owner herself, cozy and dry in a signature green vest, peeked out from behind a busy aisle of bored Washingtonians, asking if she could help. Beckett asked Gina what it would take to get into the hardware business as she ran the helium tank for us. Together, we decided he could work inventory as a side hustle because Gina would always need someone reliable for that task, and what four year old doesn't love to count.

The three of us had a moment that day and created a fond memory. We weren't having a transaction, but an experience that left an impression. Gina was delivering a best-in-class, hyper-local, high-touch service. No matter how awkward it was to head north with a bouquet of balloons on a city bus, I was sold. Even better? I snagged some local sweet treats at the front of the store where she features DC-area makers, giving them prime real estate in their own hometown. That's a differentiator.

Flock is the property management version of a reliable crosswalk monitor on a bad weather day. We're interested in relating to our stakeholders and creating relationships with them by delivering a stellar service that gets better over time. However simple the principle is, we start and finish every email with a salutation because we appreciate the same and we're selling a human experience. Because humans live in homes. Humans create communities. Looking back, it's easy to diagram how we made a business out of this philosophy.

It's been memorialized here to be of value to anyone interested in using our approach to starting, running, (and restarting) and changing a profitable, justice-based business.

We didn't know what the future held when we got our start because the problems we were solving were in constant flux. It wouldn't have been possible to create a ten-year business plan and find our way to anything resembling Flock today. It also would have been a waste of money and resources because operating with a lean startup model allowed us to be iterative and intentional at once, testing our product (and spending) as we went rather than predicting (and spending prematurely) where we would land. Our strategy was efficient because we were testing short-term hypotheses that helped us build long-term success. This included branding concepts, pricing models, grassroots ad campaigns, and demographic assumptions. When something didn't pan out, it was typically easy enough to let it go. The losses were inconsequential, even for a hungry little start up. What differentiated us practically, tactically, or fundamentally gave us an edge against our competitors, and justice was chief among these distinctions. However, building a just and purposeful company wasn't a hypothesis we were testing. It was an imperative. We were unabashed in our belief that people and place had to come before profit. It was our frame of reference, our set point, our north star.

We made it our purpose to manage homes and tend to our community because we know happy dwellers and homeowners cultivate neighborhoods and economies that are strong, sustainable, equitable, and robust. Our purpose and justice orientation inform everything we do and how we do it because we also know purpose leads to profit. Once you have a viable company or concept in view, you should look at your purpose as a three-dimensional component of your organization. It doesn't need to be complicated. Your contribution to justice might be advancing environmental sustainability, developing low-impact supply chains, or creating job pathways for underserved, underemployed communities. The most important thing to remember is that justice shouldn't be adjacent to your business; it needs to be embedded. Your clients will appreciate the difference and your team will, too.

We competed with other management companies known for being impersonal, inefficient, disorganized, resistant to innovation, poorly regarded, and disinterested in community building. To me, they were managing houses, not homes. We turned that model upside down, but our approach didn't attract customers out of the gate. It's a pain to transition management companies, which meant we had to appeal to folks new to the space or those so dissatisfied with their experiences as owners/investors, they knew they would get greater value (and benefit from better values) by moving to Nest.

Earlier, I talked about consumer choice, recognizing that consumers have an abundance of options—and not in a good way. Brands and the businesses behind them are constantly competing for our dollars. Social media is culling our preferences and serving each of us a custom feed of targeted advertisements for just what we were thinking we "needed," whether that's shoes, mattresses, or performance-enhancing medicine. We can choose from a seemingly endless number of services, products, and tools, all of which are doing all they can to compete for our attention. This is true for franchised management companies, like Renter's Warehouse, which offers discounted, flat-rate services in a quest for quantity over quality, often undercutting the mom-and-pop shops and appealing to the clients more focused on their profits and loss statements than anything else. But we knew there was a client base interested in aligning themselves with a company that's truly differentiated. Consumers want to stand out, too. If our business model offered a differentiated, attractive, intriguing, high-quality service with a high-quality portfolio of properties that were showcased like homes, the smart investors among us would prefer to be in their company rather than bundled with a group of properties that showed up in global searches with a set of photos that almost always include curtains drawn and the toilet seat up. You don't have to be good at math to understand that you might not be attracting top dollar for your property with that marketing "approach."

The home management industry has a lot of players, and there is plenty of competition among small mom-and-pop shops, the rare mid-sized companies like us, and those retail chains that offer less for, well, less. We were offering a substantially different service, but we needed to introduce ourselves to the marketplace as the only choice for a sophisticated client, rather than one among many.

To find out how to stand out, we studied the commonalities among our competition. Then we did the opposite from both a service and a marketing perspective. We put our bird on it. We rode the wave of the popular 2011 hipster Port-landia skit where Carrie Brownstein and Fred Armisen march into a gift shop to "spruce things up and make them pretty" by painting, stenciling, embroidering, and sticking birds on everything from teapots to suitcases. We gently mocked the commodification of the bird in American consumer culture because who doesn't like birds? Count us in. Thanks to that fortunate Portlandia timing, our company started to emerge as a recognizable brand when suddenly everyone was "putting a bird on it!" Lucky us. We responded with mock videos about our own bird about town and leveraged video and social media to introduce people not just to our brand, but to our team, our culture, our humor, and our value system, which is grounded in justice.

LET'S CHAT! SPEAKING IT INTO EXISTENCE

When we started out, Jim and I were doing all the things, all the time: management, maintenance, marketing, meetings on meetings, and learning lessons the hard way. On perfect spring evenings and always on Saturday mornings, we were on the run with no time to spare. Our trunks exploded with cleaning supplies and tools, and we kept telling each other and ourselves that as we got the hang of things, the work would get easier. It would slow down. Famous last words.

Washingtonians are no strangers to hard work. It's a town of deeply committed professionals, burning the midnight oil, but many can be found brunching on the weekends. Not us.

Friends sipping mimosas and Bloody Marys would look at Jim with pity when they saw him rushing down the sidewalk with a canister vac and tile saw in tow. "Jim seems stressed!" they said. "We're worried for him."

"Don't be!" I always replied. "It will all even out. Best opportunity of our lives. The work is a blast!!!"

Since we were spending as much time doing the work as selling it, there were certainly days when it all seemed fruitless. It felt like we could make more money painting and vacuuming apartments than we could "selling" the service.

In those early days, I asked people in the real estate industry and other service-based businesses how they built a reputation and grew. They said, "Meet with people as early and as often as you can." So we did. Jim and I would have lunch, dinner, coffees, or happy hours with anyone in the real estate industry and would talk to anyone marginally interested in or adjacent to our work. We talked to lawyers in the space (like our good friend Patrick Blake), commercial real estate developers, general contractors, agents, and more.

Looking back, I'm impressed that people took the time to meet with us. We had passion and a promise that we excelled where all others in the industry failed, but we really didn't have much of a story to tell beyond the experience I brought to the business managing my own handful of rentals. And I managed most of those spaces with a naive lack of information about the legal and technical requirements for doing the work well. This "jump in without a plan" approach is par for the course for me. I don't care for instructions because I find them both complicated and discouraging. Over time, attention to and appreciation for details would be precisely what I needed to hire for and seek in other team members. In the meantime, my enthusiasm and intense drive to make this idea work was enough at the start. We could fill all the details in later, with the right talent.

Still, the many, many meetings we set up rarely yielded a client, and we needed those badly. Our efforts to build an audience and attract customers sometimes meant getting comfortable with a bit of "fake it 'til you make it method" and speaking our value into existence. It's a good thing I like telling stories and an even better thing that Jim lights up every room he walks into.

We have often been asked what our secret sauce was as we set up shop. Beyond our justice-driven core values, there was another strategy that worked out nicely as we tried to build a client base: declaring early on that we were, without a doubt, the best in the business. We knew we could be—never mind that we were lime green and didn't have much relevant experience outside of my landladying and related home-maintenance skills. In those early days, we had no strategies for scale or systems that would allow us to grow gracefully. We did, however, have a north star: the "all in" service approach we favored over the "less is more" model most residents and clients were accustomed to. That was a winning investment. So was our commitment to an aesthetic.

Traditional industry branding wasn't for us. Even a cursory review of what was being used in the field left much to be desired. If we were, on some level, selling style, we needed a style-forward identity people wanted to align themselves with. We wanted a brand and imagery that made them want to sit closer, learn more, and share with their friends. Differentiation has a role to play even here, at the most granular level. Take logos, for example. In the real estate industry, I would guess that 95% of my peers have a logo with... wait for it... a house and/or key theme. I hate to be indelicate, but the field's creativity really ends there. Can you build a bold brand in a boring, stale industry? Absolutely. I would argue that for this model to work, for your company to differentiate, building a bold brand is imperative. Having chosen a field that is both deeply disliked and, frankly, boring— despite being ubiquitous—provided us with almost endless opportunities to stand out.

Only having a handful of properties to attend to in the beginning gave us a strategic advantage over our peers as well. Doing everything better is easy when you don't have many clients to answer to, and the upside of small-dollar contracts is their natural efficiency. You can't get too bogged down in them. This created a picture window of opportunity for us to design our business from scratch.

Starting with a small client base also meant we were able to cultivate a brand identity like no other in the industry. Even our name told a different story. Nest, our inaugural brand, was intentionally intriguing in its identity. Our quail pays homage to both freedom and the bird we admired most from our desert days. We took the sensibilities deployed in the real estate sales space and applied them to our own portfolio, opting to invest in high-quality photography and light staging of spaces before we listed them. We wanted residents to feel a sense of longing when they browsed our listings and clients to understand that working with us was an exclusive proposition. We positioned ourselves as city experts delivering exceptional client experiences and worked to be everything traditional landlords weren't: stylish, approachable, sophisticated, community-focused. We hit Facebook hard, did open houses, networked, and kept our fees reasonable to build a quick book of business.

Our best move in those early days happened in year two when we made a play to win *DC City Paper*'s "Best of" nod in their property management category. We only had 18 properties at the time, so we had to get creative. As someone with an abundance of grassroots organizing experience, I knew how to build a campaign, even if I wasn't sure how to manage a full-sized portfolio. Plus, coming from the nonprofit world, I was keenly aware of how much people love free things—especially tote bags. We pushed out pleas for votes in exchange for an adorable, organic tote bag. And we put a bird on it. The bags, including shipping, meant we were spending about ten dollars per vote. It was a sleepy category at the time, and the combination of strategy and luck got us to the top spot that year. Local residents took notice, and we added 80 properties to "the board"—a growing wall of glass, Ikea whiteboards where we tracked our listings. We still keep those boards populated with thousands of addresses, and today, they reflect light as they take up an entire wall of one of our offices. I get excited every single time I walk by them, even though they no longer serve any useful purpose. Eventually, we figured out that using glass Ikea whiteboards to track and manage our portfolio—and the endless number of activities needed at each site—was seriously inefficient. But there's something to be said for keeping your project management prototypes around for nostalgic reasons. Even Wells Fargo has a stagecoach in the lobby.

That was a pivotal time for Nest. The future began to come into focus, and we started seeing our "birds in the wild." A tote bag tossed over the shoulder of a shopper only reinforced our marketing strategy, particularly when folks would send photos of our then branded Mini Cooper or totes around town. We were showing up and standing out. Even if people weren't sure what we were all about, they wanted to know more. We were eager to tell them. We sent a weekly "Nestletter" that profiled what was happening in the city, offered insights on local and national politics, and, when Trump was elected, tips for modern activism (a repurposed section that had formerly been known as "Tips for Modern Dwelling"). Have some folks been turned off by our unapologetic, politically-forward business model? Absolutely. They can opt out while we self-elect to make change. Because consumers have choices, we're just making it clear why they would (or would not) choose to do business with us.

Within a year of our first win in the *City Paper*'s "Best of" issue, our investment in culture, fair compensation, and being a purposeful business had started paying big dividends. In 2013, business was thriving. We found ourselves in a new space where we had a bit more room for the dog sofa and staff at the same time. We were perched on the top floor of a former three-unit apartment building. Our new Nest home (in what had once been a two-bedroom apartment with high ceilings) was a street front office in a neighborhood where we managed a growing number of units. Our visibility and credibility as a company was solidifying. We were growing, and the team was getting increasingly sophisticated about building systems that supported our growth.

The space featured our very own photo copier, a phone system, and the constant smell of hamburgers. We were above a bar. But even with the aroma of grease frying in the background, we were deploying top-of-the-line industry software and beginning to create departments. Talented field technicians relieved me of my painting jobs as well, though I would argue I'm still the best painter the company has ever had. (A business coach once told me, after I declared the same about being a phenomenal client service rep, that if I was so good at the role, perhaps I should apply. Point taken.) I saw that to grow the company, I had to grow out of working on the things that came easily and puzzle through the more complex elements of the business.

Around that time, our quest to "get legit" started to come into focus, as did the likelihood of me being able to give the company my full-time energy. Meeting with my chief operating officer one afternoon, we went through our daily routine of asking the same questions: *Can we pay the rent? What about insurance? Payroll? Benefits? Will there be money to give as a bonus to teams at the end of the year? Is the van about to break?*

Do we need tools? That afternoon, we had a better handle than usual on the aggregate value of our growing portfolio. It took a long minute to sink in, but we saw that we had over 200 units under management. Now that they were all rented, we had a monthly cash flow that could reliably pay the staff and, at long last, me. My mind was officially blown. The sense of relief and security I felt at once was breathtaking. I had a viable business with a low probability of failing given the volume of units and the sticky nature of the contracts. This had been unimaginable just a few years prior.

Before Nest, I worked with an executive therapist after separating from a nonprofit that was a terrible fit on both sides. I was drafting a new resume, and the task felt miserable. I had no energy to wordsmith a document for who knows who, who knows where. I was tired of depending on a boss and the solvency of an organization dependent on grants. That coach advised me to spend six months ignoring the resume task, saying, "Work your fundraising side hustles for cash, and see if this property management idea you have gets you anywhere." I haven't thought about crafting a resume since. And I would prefer it if my talented staff doesn't either because, at last, our company has success in abundance. At this point, being different in the most justice-oriented way possible became even easier.

The personal satisfaction I felt in hitting a security milestone felt deeply meaningful and selfish at the same time. I recall, very distinctly, looking around the room as the magnitude of our sustainability sunk in. The team, per usual, was knee-deep in drama as they were tending to the dreams I had started sprinting toward four years earlier. How could I justify keeping this win to myself? Operating from a justice mindset, I could not. With Nest in full flight, I immediately felt inclined to share the abundance and security of its ownership. I was deeply grateful to everyone whose loyalty and hard work delivered me from the crushing weight of two jobs and the incessant vulnerability I felt as an untethered kid toggling between homes, under-resourced and under-loved. I wanted to reward that team and draw them into the magic of business ownership.

I came out of the closet about ten minutes after I got to college, but I still carried shame in two areas of my life, neither of which had to do with whom I dated. The first was my natural instinct for making money and the financial stability I built over the years. The second was being a property manager. Between lacking security and stability during my formative years and my deep ambition to be a changemaker, I have a hard time reconciling having money and working in an industry anchored in the haves and have nots. Perhaps this is what inspires the deep sense of giving back I've assigned to the work. Nothing about having financial resources and working in the real estate industry aligns with my very progressive value system. The spirit of philanthropy and giving back, plus my intentional challenges to business as usual in my industry are partly a not so subtle justification for the success I've had. Whether I like it or not, my position in society is as a wealthy white woman with a great education and an unbelievable amount of privilege.

That privilege, my hustle, and generous disposition shaped my entire relationship to business. Back in small town Hailey,

Idaho, I became quite well-known to the owners of the local antique shop for my precocious (and no doubt irritating) insistence that the rusty, vintage Yale locks I pulled from the local scrap yard were invaluable. Though I was bitter that they'd only pay me in store credit, I was able to use my earnings to shop for holiday gifts for my family. Looking back, I realize just how kind and empathetic it was of those adults to indulge a little girl's entrepreneurial spirit. They surely wondered where my parents were and why I was allowed to spend so much time in their shop. Nonetheless, they never made me feel anything other than welcome. While in many ways I consider myself a traditional entrepreneur, my interest in sharing, even through store credit, has always been more personally satisfying than keeping it for myself or even reinvesting it. Don't get me wrong: I was building a nest egg; but the extras were just that, and I recognized that investing my success in helping others paid far greater dividends to me personally. It wasn't immediately clear how this approach differentiated me, but I later understood that whatever sets you apart in business helps you stand out.

As a child, I was genuinely sated by simple pleasures like taking my family out for pizza or a splurge at the grocery store. (Could there really be a greater reward for my hard work than artichokes or Pepperidge Farm mint Milanos?) It was then that I began to recognize the personal joy I got from small comforts, and I became deeply committed to delivering that same satisfaction to others. One year, I worked on trade to put together a tall Ball mason jar full of antique marbles for my maternal grandmother. I don't know how she felt about marbles, but my grandmother spent her career working for Ball Industries in Colorado, putting together motherboards on the assembly floor. It was hard work, and I knew the jar would feel special to her. I spent a lot of time choosing experiences or gifts that showed I was paying attention to the little things that mattered to the people I loved. And I gave gifts to the many people I wanted to love me. This was a way to be seen, to be noticed. As a girl, I was awkward and unwelcome in many settings and communities without ever quite understanding why. When not selling, earning, and saving, I lacked confidence. At home, I was constantly interrupted and sometimes forgotten, so I was desperate to be noticed, respected, and looked up to at home, school, or anywhere else. Generosity gave me some of the power I lacked in my family as the youngest. The daughter. The one that came by surprise. Generosity was a way for me to deliver justice. My place in the family pecking order has improved substantially since those early days. I am changing lives because mine had changed radically with the success of Nest.

Generosity was a defining feature of every decision made when designing the businesses. It was a defining feature by design. From there, just like a jar of marbles, I composed a company that put people over profit. Even if it meant delayed or no compensation for myself. It meant giving the profits to the staff at the end of the year and designing jobs that were rich in benefits and rewards. I proclaimed early and often around the office, "My goal is to get rich and give it away!" I intended to be successful in this endeavor, but my generosity has not always led to success.

When Jim and I started Nest in 2008, I put up the funds. I delayed a salary while he drew income. I underwrote the investments we needed to make along the way and used personal funds to bring on new hires before we began drowning. Despite that, the ownership with myself and Jim was 50/50. Because "why not," I had been thinking, "it needs to be equal." Indeed, it did need to be equal. But you can't conflate equal with half.

Just a handful of years into our operations, at only 80 properties under management, I did pause to study the downsides to my generosity. Jim needed to fly the Nest and take with him, as he was entitled to do, half the value of the company. Anyone that knows Jim (myself included) wasn't surprised that dragging a canister vac down the street and pulling all-nighters to update the website and learn search engine optimization was not going to be a long-term fit. The drama, of which there is plenty in this field, continued to hold appeal for him, but the hours and lifestyle he had to live to stay responsive to our client base wasn't in the cards for him. And that was okay. Eventually. Jim needed to head back to the desert, and I needed to surround myself with a team that could help me follow my passion for business and justice guilt free and fully aligned. The time was right; we had proven our essential thesis. We confirmed a justice-driven, stylish property management company could fly high. If I could prove this theory, I wondered what more would be possible. And like the good entrepreneur I am, I got busy dreaming up something new. But this time, I had new thought partners and strong leaders on my team. And, proudly, many of them eventually became co-owners.

Since I worked for so many years in the nonprofit sector, I really like to go all-in on retreats. I'm not talking about trust falls, but instead, three-day trips to Atlantic City with meetings by day in a suite with views. By night, attendees can enjoy big dinners, drinks, and roulette. It's pretty easy to get indulgent with retreat expenses with a team of six. This became more complex (read: expensive) as Nest grew. We economized in 2013 and shared a large group house in Rehoboth, Delaware, a seaside town lots of DC gays call home during the summer. That made winter the most cost-efficient time for us to post up for a few days. In lieu of posh dinners for a small team, our larger group held a retreat kick-off at a pizza spot in town that had been recommended to us. I vaguely remember the food as being barely edible, but I clearly recall their signature "tossed" salad. It was served in a plastic bucket. The restaurant's two-for-one "mango bango" blended rum drink special made the balance of the evening much more effervescent. The next day, we gathered in a shabby living room, squeezed onto sofas and started asking aloud whether there was another bird in our "sky's the limit" future. Here I posed the question of whether an employee-owned business was a core ingredient of a justice-based economy and could provide a new future for each of us. I won't admit to the police being called during a particularly over-the-top game of Cards Against Humanity we played on the back deck of that beach house that year, but I will share that our time together changed lives.

Starting an entirely new entity helped assuage my fears around the risk inherent in co-ownership. I was smarting from the separation and the logistical complexity of buying Jim's ownership shares. Legally, tactically, and emotionally, I didn't want to take that risk again anytime soon. That risk aversion, as it had before, led to the most elegant and just option I could conceive: creating a new entity with more intentionality and shared ownership.

We roped off Nest DC and assigned it golden egg status while pursuing another business that invited employees to join as owners. Roost DC was hatched. While managing individual units throughout the District was our bread and butter, Nest had picked up a number of building associations to manage over the years. The math was compelling. DC was loaded with small-to medium-sized buildings that were host to an increasing number of Nest units, and we understood that most folks weren't pleased with their building managers. We decided to tease out that book of business and get rich as an employee-owned company.

On the face of it, starting Roost as a synergistic sister company that harmonized with the work Nest did best was the worst financial decision I ever made. At the same time, it was the most rewarding professionally. I'll unpack that a bit. I took a book of business—the condo building management work—from Nest, and we moved it into an entirely differ-ent business enterprise with a new brand, LLC, identity, and ownership structure. Any good capitalist would have kept this book of business within Nest and built greater personal net worth as a result (that scarcity bit I keep talking about). I'm not a traditional capitalist, though. I'm certain we would have enjoyed steady growth and a favorable balance sheet. But I've never been interested in a balance sheet that just favors me. In fact, I find that to be the least inspiring part of entre-preneurship. Wealth, or its potential, can be leveraged for impact at the individual level and far beyond. For me, there is no power in profits unless they are invested. Roost was such an investment.

To study the proposition in its simplest form, it's very true that Roost was a poor financial decision for me. However, the industry I'm part of is vulnerable to issues that our employee-ownership model solves. First, there's attrition and burn out, as constant churn is a significant exposure for management companies. Staff find little to motivate loyalty, given the thankless nature of the work and low-level abuse from clients and residents. It's also an industry built to lean too heavily on individual contributions versus teamwork. The portfolio man-agement model assigns a single point of contact to a client. That professional is expected to perform a symphony as a solo artist, and while there may be other players in the room, none are incentivized to support the other. An employee-ownership model turns this traditional business paradigm inside out. The incentives for growth, performance, service, reputation, excellence, and more are all co-owned. If one team member is drowning, it's simply in the best interest of the others to pull them out of the deep end as quickly as possible. It's similar to renting versus owning. Renters enjoy the freedom to come and go, but they lose out on the benefits of equity and building wealth through ownership. Conversely, owning a home comes with increased responsibility, but it offers security as well. It's a more significant proposition to buy because ownership inspires a different level of literal buy-in and commitment, whether someone is buying a house or shares in Roost.

From a consumer perspective, if someone is given a choice between working with an employee-owned company that has tenure and a solid track record and working with competition that has none of the above, we bet on the choice being obvious. We weren't wrong. Plus, it was yet another opportunity to highlight our differentiation. An attractive, forward-thinking, employee-owned business in a city bursting with politically-inclined and mission-interested Millennials has infinite potential. The new company watered down my profits in one sense, but Roost generates additional revenue growth for Nest by increasing our visibility, brand recognition, and reputation. It also gives us exposure to a large potential customer base that we don't have to market to and that gets to know us through our work.

Roost, from tailfeathers to beak, is the product of a corporate mindset that favors abundance. That design allows for more ownership, agency, and trust to emerge—all of which, when paired with a servant leadership ethos, attract more business. More business leads to greater profits when lean startup methods are employed, showing that lean operations and abundance go hand in hand. Their relationship is a differentiator.

ABUNDANCE AS DIFFERENTIATION

Being a good neighbor is one way Flock delivers justice. It's also how we show up as an alternative to the tried and tired management companies we compete with. We align ourselves with the community that supports us and, at the same time, increase our visibility and ability to create impact.

We've become quite skilled at making small community investments for high-impact wins. To make this community-based work soar—without burdening ourselves—we agreed to build a straightforward, annualized giving calendar with three areas of focus. First, we committed to pursuing volunteer activities and a certain number of hours per year. Depending on the size of the team, we could impact half a dozen nonprofits with 1,000+ hours. That isn't small change when it comes to time commitment. Second, we used our weekly newsletters, which happen to enjoy unusually high open rates in the 20%, to promote Flock and Friends, our way of spotlighting small businesses, local artists, bars and restaurants, museums, nonprofits, and our favorite—fellow purpose and justice driven companies. Newsletter content also offers our growing list of followers insider information about community activism, organizations, and local politics. And of course, weekly, we feature a delicious listing. Finally, in 2015, we decided investing our time and talent in support of our community wasn't enough to support our core values. We wanted to invest capital to walk our talk. Our team generated ideas for traditional philanthropy— through a microgrant program—without the downsides to philanthropic giving. Simply put, applying for money is a big pain in the ass for the applicant. We didn't want our giving to be a drain on anyone's time. The simplicity was essential to us as well. We had a best-in-class management service to deliver. Giving couldn't be a burden. It needed to be a net gain. Similarly, we didn't want applicants crushed with the administrative hurdles typical of the grant world. And we didn't want a nightmarish accountability model with time consuming reporting. These bureaucratic, soul-sucking activities steal precious time and energy from the people we aim to support.

We didn't have much to give, but we wanted to make it accessible and impactful. In a matter of moments, our small working group branded our philanthropic and community development efforts: birdSEED. After all, birds, growth, and germination are what we're about. The program, from branding to design to execution, harmonized with the attractive, elegant, and impactful brand we spent years developing and fine-tuning. We committed to investing $2,500 each quarter to support doers, makers, and disruptors around the District. Think community gardens, tiny libraries, supporting birthday parties for homeless kids, and floats for Dia de los Muertos parades. We hadn't seen any similar models. If companies were offering cash funding to organizations, the intent was less to make a meaningful give and instead to build a valuable mailing list by forcing "voters" to participate in the campaign with, of course, their email addresses.

For us, birdSEED wasn't released as an advertising strategy; it was an honest to goodness investment in living our values. Giving money away is a blast. And the macro was in the micro. For our cash grant program, we created an intentionally simplified application process, and we were open to people who were inexperienced, unaffiliated, under-resourced, and had no grant writing or nonprofit experience. We set out to create an inclusive giving program and set up a simple website, launched our call for applications, and gave people terms for a one-page (max) essay describing the need, budget, and project. That was it. Then we started pushing out the program through our social media, our residents, our clients, and our fans. (I'll talk about building a fanbase later in this chapter, but it certainly helps when you develop programs like this one.) The response was overwhelmingly positive. The commitment was just $10,000 a year, but the energy we got from the review process, the applicant pool, and the community felt as if this shared abundance was of a magnitude far greater than a fairly modest investment in some pretty great ideas.

Over the years, we have received hundreds of applications and have raised or donated close to $250,000. One day, we hope to grant that amount quarterly. Our rotating review committee meets and scores the applicants using an impact-analysis rubric. Typically, one project rises to the top and is a clear stand-out for funding. But for the other strong applicants, we try to pair them with support. If a musician wants to put on a show, we may not have funding available, but we'll promote the hell out of it when the time comes. If a mom-and-pop needs a bit of a storefront facelift, we may not be able to pay a company to do the work, but we can grab our brushes, rollers, and drop cloths and get it done. (One year even, Gina offered all of her "oops" paint for free if we were willing to come grab it. That wasn't a fit for the project we were working on, but we were able to find a housing organization that could relieve her of her paint mistakes.) A group of firefighters applied for a grant to install carbon monoxide and smoke detectors in homes of the elderly in underserved neighborhoods where residents might, unsafely, rely on heat from a stove. We couldn't fund their grant, but we partnered with another local hardware store to get them deeply-discounted and donated supplies. Some applicants were bringing people together, but finding meeting space can be difficult (and is rarely free) in an urban setting, particularly if you need access to a kitchen or facilities or proximity to good public transportation. We've made our office meeting spaces available to those applicants and affordable for nonprofit organizations that either lack the space or need the change of scenery our gorgeous meeting spaces provide.

birdSEED ROUND TWO

In 2021, we took birdSEED even further and established the birdSEED Foundation to add an additional focus on housing justice. The fund provides no-strings-attached down payment grants to first time homebuyers who are Black, Indigenous, or

People of Color. The magnitude of our growing understanding of how systemic racism has excluded the BIPOC community from equal pathways to home ownership led to birdSEED's Housing Justice Fund. The fund was set up with an initial investment of $215,000, and we make quarterly grants of $10,000–$15,000 per grant until the initial investment and any additional donations are fully expended. We hope that day never comes, but instead, as we turn toward a national service project, birdSEED will go wherever we do.

While I couldn't be prouder of this miracle-making and thankful to the families that have moved into their first owned homes with birdSEED's support, I have to acknowledge that our philanthropy has created a host of added benefits. For one thing, making your community better is a big-time differentiator. Just as startups rely on differentiation to win market share, so must perpetual startups maintain that practice, even when they already enjoy a substantial share of the market. Although Flock is dedicated to giving back with time and financial resources, differentiation doesn't have to increase risk or drain resources or, frankly, have anything in common with your industry. It's like a free pass to get creative and create change, or earned media but where you're the publisher. Your marketing and brand will only benefit from these distinctions between you and your peers.

We dressed up our brand by thinking of ourselves not as a property management company but as a lifestyle company with a housing niche. We didn't want a transactional relationship with our clients and residents, but something more akin to a familial relationship—with undertones of trust, reliability, and empathy. With that in mind, our marketing toolkit got really interesting. We started hosting live, large-format fund-raising events, like Casino Night, to support accessible health-care in the community. We profiled events and repurposed our office meeting and storefront spaces for cultural gatherings, pop-up shops, and very proudly, Black Lives Matter protests. We made our space available, gratis, for people convening, connecting, and coming together for community.

Our clients and residents responded with enthusiasm, as did the community in general. Why wouldn't they? We are, at a minimum, a fraternal twin with our client base when it comes to having values and politics in common. How do we know that? Because we make it a point to know them, to ask questions, to track and test what works for them. This helps us replicate successes and create economies of scale when developing outreach and marketing campaigns. What's better for a lean marketing approach—an advertisement or a community action? With the latter, you gain impact, plus visibility, reputation, relationship building, and community engagement—without the cost.

This marketing and brand strategy might sound more sophisticated than it really is. Simply put, find out what you and your audience have in common and get to work. If you're in the dry cleaning business, you and your customers might have a shared interest in environmental issues and climate change because your service uses organic products. Measure your carbon footprint and modify it. Then talk about what you did. Solar panels? Energy audits? Carbon offsets? New high efficiency products and bulbs? Then talk about it ad nauseam.

Use Facebook, Instagram, and Twitter. Snap it, Tok it, post it. Just get it out there. Write a simple, pointed newsletter to your clients (and fans) and tell them all about it. Put it on your website. Include signage in the store and offer expertise/guidance on how others might lighten their footprint at work and home. Offer referrals for solar vendors, energy consultants, or compost services. Suddenly, you have your customers and other businesses rooting for you. That's how you begin to build a fan club that extends beyond your client base. It's also an investment that pays dividends because you can talk about your values as a business. That's differentiation. That's what attracts and keeps good clients. That's what wins market share.

Don't stop angling for new ways to engage and relate to your potential customers. Urban dry cleaners are part of the fabric of urban living. They have pedestrian ease, and they often anchor city blocks and lean on neighborhood commute routines. Why not find a way to "greet" that pedestrian (or fan) with a Twitter campaign/sandwich board that gives stylish outfit tips based on what the weather has in store? It doesn't have to be complicated. Just commit yourself to meeting a need, however small, and connecting with the community you're very much a part of. Be on the minds of potential clients and fans as often as possible. Profile your clients once a month, and feature a cause or organization they really care about. Sponsor and support organizations that are meaningful to you and your client base. If you sell a product or serve a supply chain with a less engaged client base, find ways to partner with organizations that support your values and build visibility where you may not have found it. Reputation building is cost-neutral, but it serves as a form of impact investing for the company. Walk your talk and practice your values as a form of marketing. It's a winner every single time because the risk is insignificant.

Another benefit of leaning into your values and operating from a stakeholder versus a shareholder mentality is that purpose-driven, philanthropic companies that operate from just capitalism (rather than unjust and greed-based) are more attractive to consumers. Kent Gregoire, who in 2020 became the seventh certified Conscious Capitalism consultant in the world, shared with *Inc. magazine* that "nine in ten Americans now expect companies to do more than make a profit, conscious businesses perform ten times better than their peers. Conscious Capitalism is not only the right thing to do, but it's also the smart thing to do. It is now rightfully becoming both a force for good and a key comparative advantage for companies."[33] Plus, your brand recognition and visibility improve when your work isn't only associated with your product but also with your footprint and role in the world. It's an elegant and generous marketing tool.

Elegance doesn't require complexity, though. In fact, true elegance revels in simplicity. Let's talk about walking the talk again. Go on an actual trash walk. Pick a part of town that needs it, put on the company hoodie, and grab some gloves.

---

[33] Entrepreneurs' Organization'. "The Proven Methodology for Running a Successful Business Sustainably and Prosperously with the Greater Good at Heart."

It's a showstopper activity, I promise. Seeing dozens of folks in company shirts patrolling the streets while engaging in competitive trash pick-up is really something. It's one of my favorite activities, with all the good vibes you get from the unsolicited smiles and thank yous. We end our quarterly walks at a local restaurant for a long handwashing and a quick bite. If trash isn't risky enough and you care to structure your theoretical dry cleaning business around values while also making calculated bets, consider this suggestion: Tell people how to care for their clothes to reduce the need for dry cleaning by say, 50%. Halving profits might sound wildly counterintuitive, but you could always charge a little more. Plus, my inner entrepreneur guesses most folks probably won't change their dry cleaning patterns because we're all creatures of habit. That hypothetical dry cleaner has become an industry-disruptor by shifting consumer expectations around a service. At the same time, your company is aligning customers (and fans) on issues that matter. It's elegant, and it moves the needle.

We've never missed an opportunity to talk about what matters to us as a company. We're loud and proud about how we act on our values. We decided to offer paid time off for volunteering or board service. When a team member wanted a pop-up space for his clothing line that promoted a positive worldwide vibe, it was easy to not only make the space available but also promote the shop. We raised money to buy meals from struggling restaurants and then delivered that food to frontline workers weekly throughout the first quarter of the pandemic. And our fans—the people who follow us and retweet us and are neither clients nor residents—were highly responsive. That's because it wasn't just the customers we wanted to cultivate, it was also the people who like what we're all about—our fans.

Fans can be future or past patrons. They can be friends and family. Fellow business owners and industry contacts should be fans, as should vendors and neighbors. All of them. The organizations you support should, naturally, become really big fans. But fans fade if you do. So, engage them. Keep them informed and smiling. Keep them rooting for you. And they will. Because if they resonate with your values, they'll want you to fly high. That's good for business and your reputation.

Just before I wrote this section, I corresponded with a client who is a staff favorite. Earlier in the week, she shared the news that she needs to leave our portfolio. Pandemic realities and a job snag made her rental impossible to keep when she was upside down every single month. I could have wished her well and said simply, "We'll be here for you when you need us." Instead, I inquired where her career was taking her and asked if there was anything I could do as a thought partner. Career coaching was her next professional destination, and she wanted to talk through being a purpose-based business and a thoughtful consumer. I paired her with a stellar Black real estate agent, providing an opportunity for her to spend with her values and support Black business owners. Then I asked if I could connect her to the business coach we'd been working closely with for years, who produced magical management outcomes for our emerging leadership. Introducing my coach with my client was a quick but meaningful way to make connections and support two fellow business owners. Here's the

fun part: The executive coach is a former, happy Nest resident in a Roost-managed building. This is how you build brand
reputation—through authentic, empathic relationships.

With our connections, resources, and tenacity, we try to
help as many people and businesses as possible. Notably, we
give Flocksters the opportunity to self-select projects and
programs they support during work time—whether that's volunteering for a food insecurity program or raising money for
an organization that plants trees. This creates more engagement opportunities for the birdSEED Advisory Board, and our
entire Flock family, and gives the whole of the work more
meaning. This lets us play a critical dual role in the lives of our
team members. We can meet their need to grow, advance
careers, and build security and a future while also catering to
what we hope is a human instinct: to make a difference in the
world, no matter the path.

Purpose, justice, and commitment to the work go hand in
hand. Decades of studies have shown that the people most
satisfied with their work are those who find a fundamental
match between their employer's values and their own.[34] This
is especially true when the values have special moral, philosophical, or spiritual significance. For example, a 2012 study
on Iranian nurses found that the happiest ones believed
their work was "a divine profession and a tool by which they
could gain spiritual pleasure and satisfaction."[35] Many of my
colleagues feel the same way about the vocation of higher

---

[34] Ren, "Value Congruence as a Source of Intrinsic Motivation," 94–109.
[35] Ravari, Bazargan-Hejazi, Ebadi, "Work Values and Job Satisfaction:
A Qualitative Study of Iranian Nurses," 448–58.

education, and as the late philosopher Michael Novak wrote, that sense of a calling can be found in business, as well.[36]

For me as an entrepreneur, philanthropy and business must be intertwined. If we're focused on being agents of change, even as we pursue profit, the result can be profound. Businesses can wield exceptional influence as change agents. What if, instead of only measuring profit in dollars and cents, we expanded our metrics? At Flock, we concern ourselves with the number of good, secure, benefits-rich careers we support. We create paths to wealth generation for our team members and their families by offering ownership stakes in the company. We consider ourselves profitable when we carve out—and protect—time for staff to meaningfully engage in community work with their time and their unique talent. It may seem counterintuitive to lead with generosity, but the long game is an increased bottom line—and the triple bottom line is a richer one. Philanthropy is part of that investment. It also creates positive outcomes beyond the purely altruistic since it can help businesses become far more successful. This is because purpose-driven, justice-oriented companies generate increased buy-in and genuine engagement from employees, which reduces turnover, increases productivity, improves overall job satisfaction, accelerates recruitment, and strengthens the culture. All of that is likely to lead to greater profits and buttresses the justification for shared abundance. Profit should not be used as an entitlement but leveraged as an act of justice.

---

[36] Novak, *Business as a Calling.*

PART FIVE

CHAPTER 10

PEOPLE + THE CULTURE OF SERVANT LEADERSHIP

LEADING FROM BEHIND, AHEAD, AND BESIDE

Servant leadership paired with a purpose-driven business is a natural philosophical marriage, which explains its popularity among organizations and companies that are mission based.

Both a practice and an approach, it is particularly relevant and effective in a service based organization that relies on human talent to deliver a best-in-class experience. Traditional hierarchical models privilege a top-down management approach that places power in the C-suite. Servant leadership eschews power grabbing in favor of power sharing. The most effective servant leaders operate "in service" to their teams. This approach cultivates stronger, more robust, and more collaborative teams. And it's a model that has penciled out nicely for our family of companies.

One approach to servant leadership is to feature your staff. Let them lead and represent the company in different ways. Servant leaders don't need to be out front. There's room for plenty of folks to have signature authority and represent the company. That's where you cultivate a strong leadership bench because, with the right people and a shared vision, you can operationalize every area of your business more effectively. You will have more highly functional teams with the ability to design and implement complex systems and solve complicated problems.

To deliver on this model, service leadership tells us not to just give talent and teams a voice, but to actually listen to them. Service leadership also recognizes that we don't just manage talent, we manage humans. Developing a staff with staying power requires supporting their work, as well as their lives. That's the only way to create just, life-changing jobs. And without that philosophy, you risk having a revolving door of talent.

I wanted to create a one-of-a-kind workplace with game changing, once-in-a-lifetime jobs that not only kept people with the company, but also kept them thriving. Early on in the company, I thought long and hard about turnover. I wanted to create a work home that was so cozy, inviting, and inspirational that the right talent never felt inclined to spread their wings and leave. But as someone running a company with a theme related to flight and freedom, this didn't sit right with me. So rather than clipping wings, we created professional flight paths within our family of companies. Property management is a static field; it is often lacking in innovation and upward mobility for anyone but the owner and perhaps those on a senior leadership team, if there is one. For our Flock, being in a constant state of organizational evolution generated opportunities for staff to make significant career changes without leaving the nest, so to speak. By building on and expanding our business model, we mined the brain trust we'd worked so very hard to cultivate. My instincts here appear to be borne out by data. Ryan Jenkins, a columnist for *Inc.* who focuses on generational differences, found that "75% of Gen Z would be interested in a situation in which they could have multiple roles within one place of employment."[37] Even so, the approach mattered, and it was clear that mapping opportunities on their behalf wasn't the answer. The best approach, we found, was to convene that team and learn from them what came next. We couldn't thrive as a company unless we were all flying in formation.

I'll admit there is some degree of anxiety that comes with this. If I really want my team to take flight, I have to be willing to push them out of the nest. Several years ago, I joined a global community of successful (to varying degrees) business founders and owners, the Entrepreneurs' Organization (EO). There's a helpful baseline commonality within the network,

---

[37] Jenkins, "Statistics Exposing What Generation Z Wants from the Workplace."

and even though I'm the only lesbian in my local chapter and one of only a small fraction of women (19%) there, EO provides me with a peer group I can compare myself to, contrast against, and commiserate with. The EO model encourages leaders not to work *in* their businesses but rather *on* their businesses—to, in other words, be willing to push the birds out of the nest and not be home when they get back.

That journey requires, at first, a leap of faith, and not just for the baby birds. Nobody can parent a company like the momma bird. Nonetheless, as the company moves through different stages of growth, there are simply areas of oversight where the founder becomes a cog, not a conduit. If my true value is to bring vision, inspiration, and momentum to the organization, getting snagged in details and deliverables is a disservice to the company and my team. I had been brave enough to surround myself with tremendous talent. The solution was to trust them to lead.

Consequently, in 2017, I moved from a two-person leadership model and created the Flock Leadership Team. This group was charged with handling the lion's share of client-facing work, systems oversight and implementation, and almost all operations. They weren't ready for it, as baby birds rarely are, but they were eager to get there. We worked hard on this transition together, using the guidance of a coach to become comfortable with our roles, relationships, and shared expectations for the growth of our wingprint. Pulling myself out of the day-to-day needs meant fewer immediate wins, but it also meant leaning into my instincts to trust the team surrounding me. The bet paid off and continues to pay off, but for the proposition to remain viable, we have to evaluate and adjust the model constantly. That requires a lot of focus, a lot of discipline, and a lot of time. It also makes us far more efficient than we would be otherwise.

While not everyone is capable of excelling in an empathy-based business, those who can and who rise to leadership are consistently high performers within the organization. Our Flocksters are truly committed. A reporter with the *Washington Post*, Thomas Heath, who did a story on Flock in 2019 put it this way: "I recently spent an afternoon with the Flock and instantly noticed the relaxed, conversational club-house-like vibe. Everyone seemed serious about the job, but they also seemed happy."[38] This satisfaction comes, in part, from knowing that I have their backs; that the business will take care of them.

This holds true even when that means parting ways with a client. I believe the client is king—but that queens have more value. The team who cares for our client base is made up of hardcore, take-no-prisoners, problem-solving queens. In a service-based industry, it's so important not to take for granted the value each member brings to the job itself, the client experience, and the overall success of the company. If I couldn't take care of my talent—my queens—then how in the world could I deliver for our client base? And if taking care of our talent sometimes meant severing ties with abusive clients who hid behind their keyboards and emailed to make us miserable every day? Well, that was a king who needed to be

---

[38] Heath, "Managing Real Estate, Building Wealth."

taken off the board. The sanity of our staff will outweigh losing the business of a bully every single time.

Once, early on at Nest, I started to sense tension between our staff and a select number of clients who, no matter the issue or our effort to resolve it, couldn't be satisfied. These were owners whose expectations were always out of reach and with whom we were in a constant state of negotiation. The kind of client that could ruin a day and an appetite for the career. I needed the team to know I work for them first, clients second.

So one day, almost on a whim, I grabbed a piece of paper, ripped it into strips, and handed a piece to everyone in our office. (By "our office," I mean that space above the bar that smelled like hamburgers all the time.) I asked everyone to jot down the names of clients they wanted to fire. Within the week, we had terminated 15 contracts. We needed every one of those contracts to survive financially, but I knew that with them we would fail every day. I also realized that spending time with the clients and residents who valued our work would inevitably lead to more work. As our office location suggested, this was in the days before we were stable enough to offer strong salaries, but my bet that we would replace bad clients with better ones paid serious dividends when it came to our organizational culture. Parting ways with clients helped solidify our commitment to people and place over profit.

We needed to understand not all business is good business. And it was in our best interest to study early and often those clients who did not align with our values, workflows, or partnership standards.

Just as I was coming to the finish line on the first draft of this book, we hit a very similar growing pain with Roost DC. That business tends to community associations or condo buildings (COAs), and this is a particularly delicate time for the condo world. As a specialist in the field, I anticipate a legislative and economic shift in how condominium associations and home-owner's associations (HOAs) operate and contribute to the American real estate landscape.

Washington, DC's housing landscape is a unique mix of row houses, single-family homes, and a growing number of condo developments throughout every quadrant. Some buildings are condo conversions sparked by the 1961 National Housing Act, which was passed to increase affordable housing stock. Other communities are newer, and many are former single-family rowhomes expanded to host two or more units. No matter the size of the building, there are specific operational, facility, governance, and financial obligations that need to be met. Every condominium is required to have a board of directors, and they ensure the building is well managed from a financial, governance, and facilities perspective. Every owner in a building has some responsibility in overseeing property management and long-term planning for the building's common and limited common elements. The board is elected by the ownership to manage the affairs of the building. Those board members volunteer their time and, depending on the age, resources and personalities in any given building; it's a big lift with no pay and has a significant impact on the building's future and the day-to-day quality of life for residents. The tragic collapse of Champlain Towers South Condominium in Florida during the summer of 2021 underscores the critical importance of maintaining buildings and stewardship of the community. The work of a board is essential, yet working with a condo association's board of directors can be extremely challenging.

In the DC market, condos make up a sizable number of small buildings around the city, with unit sizes commonly ranging from two to 40. What's also common is the lack of resources and support available to communities working to establish themselves or ensure best practices are being followed. Even though legally, they are obligated to do so, governing and managing a building doesn't come with a manual, and there is a lot of room for error, hurt governances, and outright, if unintentional, law breaking. Further, the financial due diligence needed for every community can be overlooked or not prioritized. This oversight leaves many buildings without sufficient financial reserves to maintain the property properly. Roofs often need replacement, or the building might have leaking hot water heaters or be situated atop shifting foundations. The 100-year-old masonry is crumbling on many of the historic buildings. But many condo owners are just beginning their lives as homeowners and are unprepared for (or, in the worst cases, disinterested in) ensuring the long-term wellness of their building. That creates a "kick the can" dynamic for many owners and buildings. Many buyers live in their units for a few years as the value appreciates, particularly in the first five years barring unusual economics, and then once they are no longer subject to capital gains, they move on to something bigger or better, leaving the long-term care and preservation of the building to the next buyer or the buyer after that. There is little incentive for most owners to honor their role as stewards of the building. Most condo dwellers are (not unreasonably) most focused on their personal and short-term needs unless a problem is immediately impacting the property value. The problem is, while it may not be unreasonable, at some point, it becomes downright unrealistic. Yet this isn't an uncommon dynamic in the DC marketplace and beyond, and it has made me wonder who will be left footing the bill when these deferred maintenance needs outpace the building's rising property value. Someone, somewhere down the road will be left with an asset worth less than it is on paper, as with the people in coastal Florida who own condos they can neither live in nor sell. Without policy changes and industry-wide pressures to resolve this looming threat to US housing stock, we have another housing crisis on the horizon. That's a potential threat to the nation's economy, consumers, and the communities hosting those condos.

As a day-to-day practice, most condo-owners are blissfully unaware, intentionally ignoring, or simply disinterested in how their home is in a precarious state of being because their community has an alarming lack of resources and no plan. Yet many owners relentlessly push for all kinds of upgrades and repairs to the common areas even in the absence of funds to do so. Think, "we should get a roof deck" or "we need new lobby furniture" when the reality is, their building can't really afford pest control, let alone capital improvements unlikely to meet government approval. Unfortunately, most folks aren't aware of the financial and physical constraints the building is saddled with. But they often see it as management's failure when that roof deck isn't on the agenda at the next annual meeting.

The pandemic really brought out the worst of the high-density urban dweller set. No matter what we said, many could not understand why we weren't in a constant state of "above and beyond." But they didn't know we likely lacked basic resources to do the minimum for the building. And when those "needs" weren't met, they became inconsolable in a good case and irate and abusive in the worst case. Serving those clients during a pandemic became that much worse because they had all day, every day to think about how their building might be improved (even though, of course, they didn't want anyone actually entering the building). In the end, we spent much more time on under-resourced buildings for which we couldn't deliver decent baseline service. And, because we picked up the phone, condo owners who neither understood our contract nor our role found us to blame for the building not being maintained or delays in improvements.

One day, seeing our team suffer through these no-win scenarios, navigating one escalation after another, I suggested we either shut down the whole operation or fire the hell out of our loss leaders. We could focus on the buildings that treated us and their buildings with respect. That's because we could only do good work in partnership, not under someone's thumb. We cut 20% of the business in 60 days and set about redesigning the entire business model.

We rededicated ourselves to the premise that working with us isn't a consumer guarantee; working with Roost is an exclusive opportunity for those buildings that want stellar management and are interested in investing in the future of the building, not just meeting immediate personal needs.

We were dragging as a company when I made this decision, bogged down by the never ending pandemic, increasing workload, and decreasing resources. Residents, boards, and vendors were all on the verge. The last straw after 15 months of pandemic property management? Tenley Town Garbage, a waste management company owned by a Barney Shapiro, a local hippie in the District, felt the same way we did and cashed in his trash chips. Barney sold his company out of the blue and headed, presumably, for a beach somewhere, leaving the District buried under piles of trash that the new vendor was sorely unprepared to collect. And of course, Tenley was one of the biggest vendors in town. He was perfectly aligned with us in that he had a peace sign on the side of his trucks, but peace was just a dream when, in that single transition, our business instantly got more complex. People want their garbage picked up. Period. Owners and residents were immediately suffering—only to pass that blame onto us despite every proactive communication plan we could implement. It's as if we were personally leaving the trash uncollected. Week after week, month after month. We'll let you know when we hear back from the trash company, but it's not looking good. Was it just about trash? Not at all. But to avoid something like trash being such a substantial operational threat, we needed to study our business model, systems, and service.

Our strategy has been, in the meantime, to put our Roost team first and lighten their load. I hope the 20% reduction in business is one of the very best investments we can make in a stronger future where, at a minimum, the staff knows we put their wellness and sanity ahead of profits.

To be clear, we don't get rid of contracts over any little conflict or because someone was rude on the phone. The nature of the business means we are often interacting with people when they're at their most anxious. We understand this, and we handle emergencies with grace day-in and day-out. The floods, lockouts, small fires, break-ins, and other unexpected events keep work interesting. We're accustomed to helping clients through distressing times, and everyone comes out happier on the other side. The clients we've fired have been exceptional—and not in the complimentary way.

Several years ago on one Friday night (and it's almost always a Friday night), we received a call from three young women sharing a 100-year-old house in northeast DC. They had locked themselves in the bathroom. This was because a raccoon had found its way into the house and, in doing so, cut itself badly. Then, in its desperate efforts to exit the house, the creature proceeded to bleed over pretty much every square inch of the unit. Given the behavior of the raccoon, we had to assume it was rabid. Like all client problems, we set about solving this one with a smile and had a technician on site in 90 minutes. He chased the raccoon out of the home, liberated the tenants from the bathroom, and had the young women relocate to friends' houses for the evening. He then called an environmental cleaning company to safely address the bio-hazard. After committing to about $8,000 for the cleanup/remediation (and discovering how profusely raccoons bleed), we were able to get the residents back into their home. All the while, we kept the owner up to date in real time about the status of the emergency, our resolution, and his responsibility for the raccoon breach. While we updated the owner by calling and writing as all this unfolded, we received no response from him during the thick of things. But our sense of right and wrong—and the contract—gave us the latitude to act ethically and quickly, so we did just that.

Naturally, we felt so heroic, we reached for our capes. Our valiant efforts brought no comfort to our client, however. He not only disagreed with our approach, but he also blamed us for the raccoon's break-in since we hadn't sealed off access to the unit. (This is despite the fact that he specifically asked us *not* to perform maintenance on the property since he would personally handle issues to economize before renting it out.) He also somehow held us responsible for endangering the lives of the tenants. So there we were, knowing we did the right thing morally and legally to protect the residents (and the owner) and nonetheless finding ourselves staring at an $8,000 bill, an angry vendor, and an owner threatening a Yelp attack. We were getting crushed by unforeseen events that I knew we'd handled well.

I tell the team that I'll do anything to save a client relationship, but I knew there would always be exceptions. I would not preserve a client relationship at the expense of our flock. It was a hard lesson, but a valuable one. It was important for me to recognize that I couldn't rely on our clients and residents to appreciate our hard work and commitment to delivering the best outcomes. Instead, I needed to budget for bullies and irrational behavior. When dealing with people's homes—typically their largest asset—and their wallets, the role of a property manager becomes suspect and invites endless second guessing. It's no wonder most property managers choose to deliver the most baseline service and take a pass on a customer-forward approach to the work. When clients don't begin by assuming the best, it's unlikely we will convince them otherwise, and the time and energy invested in doing so stops penciling out after a while. I could either lower the caliber of our service to protect us from delivering time-consuming experiences that were underappreciated, or I could double down on our commitment to service and divorce clients who couldn't appreciate our model. I chose the latter. I have no interest in delivering mediocrity just because it's the path of least resistance.

CHAPTER 11

PURPOSE
IN PARTNERSHIP

If business is going well, at least in our industry, we're not just working for clients, we're partnering with them. Per the contract, each of us plays a role in delivering positive outcomes and managing and/or avoiding crises. In a non-productive, toxic relationship with a client, there is often a winner/loser subtext that can begin to dominate conversations and muddy waters when working on projects. When this happens and when the relationship is soured and the client can't find their way back to a respectful collaboration, you, at first, gently nudge them toward a reset—whatever the reason. If they don't have a reset button on their keyboard, you firmly and fairly remind them of their contractual obligations. If they choose to pursue a 10x return on their toxicity investment, you should give your team, as I do, full permission to fire their asses because making a living while being abused doesn't inspire loyalty, hard work, or buy-in from your team. It inspires turnover and all the reputational and financial expenses associated with it.

Remember, in a service-based business, your first partnership is with your staff, not your client base. In stark and illuminating contrast, when boldly and unapologetically doing what's right for your staff, no matter the cost, your culture will be unbeatable. Growth will heat up with the right loyalties. Sir Richard Branson said, when asked if his success was because he put customers first, "Clients do not come first. Employees come first. If you take care of your employees, they will take care of the clients." I think we can agree that approach penciled out nicely for the stakeholders he answered to.

One of my proudest moments as a leader came mid-pandemic, watching from the electronic stadium and cheering on a senior level Roost director we hired and onboarded during the pandemic while he dueled a "spirited" client to the finish. Jason came to us with a decade of industry experience because he wanted room to grow, direct, and build his own leadership brand. He heard on the (industry) streets, Roost was the place to do just that. He was right. And we got lucky.

Just nine months into his tenure, Jason observed an increasingly volatile client relationship that was not only sour, it was soul crushing for his direct reports managing that building, which had taken a turn for the worse when their volunteer board of directors all resigned and a new board came, well, on board. Expectations were misunderstood, there was a major point of disagreement, and nobody on the new board wanted to mind the contract terms. Condescending, unclear, misinformed, cruel, and passive (if they bothered with passive) correspondence memorialized the misery of our work with them. Jason—with full company support—wrote the following:

> Mr. Jill and Ms. Jack: Your email communications have devolved into an onslaught of abusively worded demands, passive aggressive follow ups, unnecessary capitalizations, and to be blunt: are out right disrespectful. And while you all should have every expectation of a positive client experience, our team members should be able to maintain a positive work environment. If this type of communication is what our team can expect, I will move to termination negotiations. I will not have Ms. A, Mr. B, Ms. L or any Rooster subjected to this.

I'm certain the book on how to write a business book would very explicitly forbid the writer from quoting staff email as illustrative of the company value system. Well, call me a rule breaker because this direct, candid, and professional reply reflects our core values as a company; we put our people over profit. And Jason, in a handful of sentences, honored not only this value, but he reinforced our reputation and practices as a company that indeed honored the client experience, but not at the expense of our greatest asset, our very human talent.

Borrowing from my nonprofit management history, I brought on a small group of interns from nearby colleges. I can't say the program was always a win, but it certainly created some great stories.

One task I assigned to a green and not particularly moti-vated intern was preparing our giveaways. We made a signa-ture chocolate "nest" with dark chocolate and crispy Chinese noodles. We'd drop in little chocolate eggs. It was obvious, but sweet, and perfect for events and tucking into swag bags. We were gathering with fans at a local antique store on 14th Street, and I was ready to impress. Unimpressively, that not-so-eager intern turned every chocolate nest into what looked like dog poop wrapped in plastic. Queue the sunset of the chocolate nest. Failed recipes aside, our momentum as a team was building, and we were able to gauge quickly where things were turning to... chocolate nests, and where our strategies produced shinola.

As with the interns, I often make choices that could have been improved upon, reconsidered, or more carefully studied. That's likely why my key confidants force me to slow down and consider additional options. While I don't always value their counterpoints in the moment, I can certainly appreciate it when hindsight reveals that their deliberate, measured, and methodical approach sometimes leads to better outcomes. As our talent pool grew, I needed a deliberate, intentional, and measured work family, too—one that could offset my "jump in and swim!" style. So I set out to hire a phenomenal staff and built a team that was so impressive that they would ultimately become co-owners of our second brand, Roost.

Creating an employee-owned company is a lot easier when you're working with a stellar staff. The arc of our growth has shaped our success and reinforces just how important it is to hire well. I think we've developed processes that make such hiring possible, but there were certainly hiccups along the way. At the beginning, what worked for us from a hiring perspective was in no way sustainable as an actual codified practice. For any company not interested in accumulating debt, cheap and available talent is a non-negotiable criteria. We consequently relied on a very young talent pool to start Nest. To be candid, it was the only talent pool we could afford. Pairing my nonprofit tricks with my for-profit instincts, we introduced (improved) internships and partnered with universities across the country to get full-time talent at bargain basement prices.

In those early days, we spent most of the interview process selling the company to the candidate and not the other way around. We didn't have the resources to compensate anyone the way I would have liked, so we paid a passable hourly rate and hoped the culture and thrill of being part of something new would be enough to get a commitment. Fortunately, young people who were new to the professional world were willing to take more risks to get in the door and gain some experience.

That was a winning approach until we realized we kept overlooking skill gaps. Many on the team lacked relevant experience. Recruiting, onboarding, and hiring was a mess.

Our staffing needs outpaced our ability to formalize, stream-line, and memorialize our hiring practices. We were always behind. The end result? Bad interviews, bad hires, even worse terminations. One of my favorites: a woman who sat through the entire interview clutching her purse (as if we were about to take it) and who was only interested in what time the offices closed for the day. Yet we still wasted 30 minutes of our collective time going through the interview motions, which were ultimately a waste. Something about our for-mal screening process was failing. Maybe because we didn't have a formal screening process. As we grew, we graduated to needing staffing standards that made hiring more compli-cated. Four years after our founding and three years after our first hire, we moved from a traditional interview model (where we non-traditionally did all the talking) to a "try before you buy" approach to the task. With this lean startup meth-odology, we were testing ideas, not building out extensive systems and protocols before we knew what we needed—even when it came down to hiring. We couldn't afford the time or money to take that long-term risk, which, ironically, is less risky overall.

Using this model, we paid candidates for a specific number of hours or days, depending on the position, giving people a chance to become familiar with our culture and the tasks required for the job. We created structured tasks and activities designed to test their critical thinking and problem solving skills, as well as expose them to the kinds of client interactions they would have on any given day. People inter-ested in becoming field-based team members would ride along with tenured Nesters to help them understand the rip and run dynamics of being on the go all day—while maintaining the highest degree of accountability to our clients and to the company's reputation. This had the added benefit of giving candidates a chance to interview us and understand what the company is all about. This legacy hiring practice continues to serve us well.

Another Flock convention that has proven fruitful has been our commitment to enthusiastic hiring of the most disrespected of generations: Millennials. We Gen Xers may have cornered the market on parental absence, but our upbringings were at least thought to have turned us into independent, self-sufficient adults. We were shaped by a range of worries, from 1980s interest rates and the designation of ketchup as a vegetable to 9/11 and the Great Recession. For years, I lived with the certainty that my family and I would be leveled, either by a nuclear bomb or another layoff. But all this insecurity and uncertainty made me empathetic. And it gave me grit.

Grit is currency in life, not to mention a requirement for small business owners in the US. In the end, it's what gets us through the barriers we run up against. But when it comes to grit, my generation has nothing on Millenials, never mind Gen Z, whose opportunities are even more limited and whose anxiety is rightfully abundant. These young people have endured a housing market crash that some communities/populations have yet to recover from, crippling student loan debt that doesn't come with the silver lining of probable gainful employment, a catastrophic global pandemic, some of the highest unemployment rates the United States has ever seen, and a long overdue national reckoning on race. We may as well call them Generation Grit.

And yet, despite the historic struggles they've been through and continue to live every day, they have managed to become kind and empathetic. They understand that things are hard; they listen to and validate one another's feelings; they grasp their role as citizens of the planet and defenders of justice; and frankly (thanks to, I suspect, those much-maligned helicopter parents), they display emotional intelligence that is off the charts. This combination of empathy and grit is why, when many in corporate America were busy writing off Millennials as lazy and self-centered, I doubled down on the generation and assembled a team so loyal and sophisticated, they are with me today as we move toward national expansion and iconic status as a social justice-driven company.

In his national 2020 commencement speech, President Obama reminded the nation's graduates "to be alive to one another's struggles." In other words: *It's not all about you.* Having built a business with a team of emerging professionals, I'm here to tell you that my staff not only understands this message, but also knows how to live it. This is not the young workforce of the greed-is-good 1980s. For the most part, they are innovative, scrappy, and interested in a mission-based approach to work. The young people who have helped me build my company are akin to snowflakes only in their humble grasp of the fact that snow melts fast and survival depends upon sticking together.

To build a better and more just future, it is long past time to quit disparaging these resilient generations. After the murder of George Floyd, it was young people who were at the center of shifting the national discourse. The pandemic era has been difficult, but it has also been ripe for lifting up new ideas and fostering new leaders. I am comforted by the vision and drive of today's emerging generations. Their determination and fearlessness gives me hope for humanity. Luckily for us (and apologies to Tom Brokaw), I believe we may be looking at the two greatest generations, back-to-back, that this country has ever seen.

It's important to note that as Nest became more profitable, I didn't shift to hiring staff with more extensive property management experience. For one thing, if the goal was to break and rebuild the traditional approach to property management, what would leaning on the industry's built-in talent pool do for us? Not much. Yes, my young and eager staff was as green as it gets, and none had the experience necessary to pull off the idea of growing a company that looks like the one we have today. But we did pull it off. That's because I was willing to suspend disbelief and trust my young talent. When we brought in more money, I used it to improve pay and benefits for the people we had and attract the right, experienced talent at the right time. Industry peers criticized me for over-promoting and offering titles and salaries that weren't consistent with business standards or traditional trajectories. I didn't care. If paying well and promoting the young and the inexperienced was ill-advised, that was a risk I was willing to take. I was confident it would let me lock in passionate, hard-working, and talented team members who were willing to learn as they went and who were interested in staying with me and the company. (These days, we do attract people with industry experience, but they're the right people. They are drawn to what our earliest Flocksters helped build and equally interested in shaping a new vision for the industry. I see that as a sign of organizational maturity.)

The combination of building a team that was largely composed of Millennials and Gen Zers and that had no experience in the field meant I was surrounded by compassionate, empathetic people who weren't interested in carrying industry baggage. As I've mentioned before, there is baggage aplenty, given that property management is essentially the real estate industry's less sexy half brother. There are no champagne moments in traditional property management (though Flock finds a way). Instead there are broken toilets, leaks, fires, floods, lover's quarrels, lots of pot smoking, overgrown lawns, barking dogs, jammed garbage disposals, lockouts, and—a personal favorite—rodent infestations. We're in an urban environment, so you pick the rodent. We manage problems. Day-in and day-out. Each client contract is valued in the hundreds, not hundreds of thousands, so turning a profit means managing hundreds upon hundreds and, today, thousands of contracts in total.

To become the company we set out to be meant embracing our role as professional problem solvers. Rather than merely lament the abysmal characteristics of my chosen industry, I studied it to develop a "what not to do" roadmap for Flock. Our commitment to style and investment in branding were critical differentiators for us, as was our leadership model, culture, and willingness to innovate with technology and more. But the most striking difference between us and traditional property management was our stellar service with a smile—emphasis on stellar, service, and smile. And you don't get there with burned out, unsupported staff.

I continue to take immense pride in how my team has managed to maintain this dedication in the midst of a global pandemic. For every patient and kind client we're working with, there are several more who are on the verge. But patience and a decent sense of humor, paired with being as responsive as one can be given the circumstances, is sometimes the best we can do, accepting that spaces, like their residents and owners, are full of surprises. Case in point: One night, an emergency call came in because a resident reported her refrigerator had flames coming out of the bottom. Reasonably enough, she was worried about a threat of fire to the unit and her building. Plus there was the issue of personal danger. We asked her to send a photo/video and advised her to immediately turn the appliance off by unplugging it and to loop back that night if there were any continuing safety issues. The next day, we reached out to work on next steps. She reported that turning the refrigerator off didn't seem worth it because she had a fresh piece of salmon inside and didn't want it to go bad. There are some things we can control when it comes to reputation and client experiences and others we have to accept as less than ideal if not absurd.

It can be hard to sort out the serious from the silly, but when there are legitimate and emerging maintenance issues, we have a sophisticated system and outstanding, at the ready staff who can deliver. A few years ago, we had a tenant who moved into a unit on a Saturday and discovered that the hot water tank was broken. Dane, who has been with Flock since the early days when we were simply Nest, made sure that she had a new tank within 20 hours. Please tell me if you've ever had a major maintenance problem, as a tenant or owner, addressed so quickly and resolved on a Sunday. Because if you have, I want to hire the person who made it happen. The actual punch line? Dane was on vacation. He wasn't required or expected to address this problem. But Flocksters are professional problem solvers, delivering a stellar service, and he didn't want a client to go without hot water.

Of course, Dane cannot be all places at all times. For our first few years, meeting the high expectations of our clients often meant leaning on outside vendors with varying standards, degrees of availability, and capacity to communicate (or bill) clearly, if at all. So in 2015, we chose instead to lean on our perpetual startup philosophy and formalized our maintenance and turnover work with another bird. And a new Starling was hatched. With this brand, we positioned ourselves as a company that could create resident-ready spaces, tend to resident needs quickly and efficiently, and also leverage the service as another revenue stream if and when our own in-house needs waned. (We're still waiting for that waning.) Today, Starling crews churn and burn; painting, patching, and polishing spaces for residents or putting on capes to handle things as varied as floods, burglaries, manhole explosions, or—one of my personal favorites—a tree falling on a house and impaling two floors of the structure.

Having a highly responsive field team is one of the most important and complicated parts of our business and why building out Starling was a solid, strategic bet. That's not to say it was all wins. I'm reminded of one of my favorite maintenance techs, Doug, who was unusually available 24/7 with a perfect smile and a willingness to take on any task—provided he could be creative with whatever resources he had on hand. Meaning, he would install seasonal window units with white duct tape for that "extra touch." Long, weird story short, Doug's availability suddenly changed. One day Doug "ghosted"—before that was even a thing—and after a quick Google search, we learned he'd just been assigned to a federal prison in Connecticut for mortgage fraud, and we learned he had been waiting for his facilities assignment the whole time he was "on-call" for us. Hence the ease of scheduling his time, until suddenly, it wasn't possible at all. Another technician drywalled a cat into a ceiling. My least favorite tech used a machete to break into our locked, idling in traffic van during rush hour. And somewhere along the way, he lost track of his shoes. He wasn't long for the job. Still, for every maintenance fail, there were wins upon wins, and I was clear that having in-house technicians made us vastly better property managers. We could be highly responsive and nimble, and we could work to the standards we set for ourselves as opposed to the typical industry standard, which didn't agree with us or our residents.

The best part? Starling offers a pathway to workforce development programs. We're talking about creating good jobs for returning citizens or training opportunities for folks that aren't tracked for higher education, which is both expensive and unnecessary for many. We want to create and offer not just jobs, but life changing careers for folks from all walks of life. This is better for the worker and the world. This is where change happens. This is justice and business at once.

With three birds under our belt, a lot of questions about our work started with "What's the difference between... (fill in the blank) bird... and... the other... (fill in the blank) bird?" After a decade, it was time to answer that question. In 2018, we decided to fly in formation and combine all of our birds into one brand, Flock DC. The sky was the limit. Flock was more than a tool to create brand clarification; it also solved some of the complexities we were generating operationally and culturally. If clients wondered what the difference was between our brands, it was a safe bet there were internal disconnects as well. We were facing silos and a lack of understanding about how our brands intersected with and supported each other. As we grew, we began breaking workflows down to management areas of expertise for team members. As this happened, reminding teams of a big picture and tying their work to the mission became more challenging. Flock solved part of this identity crisis and unified our culture. It gave each of us a chance to fly in formation. It was also operationally more efficient. After incorporating, every team member became an employee of Flock, and at last, we were all a number of birds of one kind. This left ample room for our family of companies to experiment with and explore the release of new birds and business units. Because even as a justice-driven company, being growth oriented was key to our sustainability, our success, and our ability to self-elect.

EMPATHY AS A JUSTICE ENGINE

It's difficult to imagine that we could have grown as quickly as we have had it not been for our foundational commitment to supporting our staff. Even in the early days, when we tripled down on culture since we couldn't with compensation. We knew that our across-the-board focus on empathy would be a key ingredient in building and sustaining our relationships with our clients and each other. Empathy is one of those concepts that has been a through-line in my life, partly because I didn't experience as much as I could have used as a child. Now, I lead with empathy and my team does as well. Compassionate empathy is one of Flock's core values, and it's truly concerning how often we're exceptional in this regard.

Let me give you a real-life example of how empathy, or the lack thereof, can affect a relationship. I've spent more time horizontally situated in a dentist chair than anyone I know. A childhood "accident" led to a broken front tooth and subsequently, 30 years avoiding smiles. That front tooth was the bane of my existence. Despite my smile deficit, I enjoyed an unusually straight set of choppers, but no one had ever bothered to check my bite. So dozens of years of stress grinding, combined with an unaddressed cross-bite, led to an endless number of dental procedures. And with each dentist, I dreaded the relationship. I found practices and practitioners were almost universally lacking in true empathy. Pair this with the exceptionally high price tag and the pain that came with every single procedure, and it's no wonder I wasn't up for smiling. But just before I got married and just after we started Nest, I realized it was time to fix my teeth because I had a lot to smile about. A ton of research finally produced Dr. Charlie Varipapa, a perfect fit. He ran his practice out of a gorgeous row home in northern Virginia's Old Town Alexandria. He treated one patient at a time, and over the next several years, he restored my smile and my self-esteem and became someone I truly looked forward to seeing. I needed to see other specialists while working with Dr. V, and there were several occasions when a dental situation was so urgent he drove me to the specialist himself. One wintery Saturday, he met me in his office to deal with a cracked tooth. He gave me a meat thermometer that day because he said it was one of the most accurate he'd used. (He had bought them in bulk for all his patients, which was unexpectedly surprising to me since I felt like I was his *only* patient.) Dr. V. was and still is, magical. It also seemed like his practice was highly profitable. He enjoyed international travel, second and third homes, and trendy cars, and during one horizontal chat, he shared details of his 24-hour trip to Las Vegas to see Cher. I was happy to contribute to his wealth. As far as I was concerned, he deserved it. Then he retired.

When I last went to the restored row house in Old Town, Alexandria, it was buzzing with patients and assistants and printers and paperwork. More rooms were converted to patient rooms, and this seemed to quickly produce the set-up I've always loathed about dentistry. Churn and burn. More patients, more money. Dr. V's successor didn't bother to connect with his patients. (I'm talking about no eye contact or *how ya doin'*? kind of bother). I broke a tooth, and it took three weeks to get in. I waited 50 minutes in a chair before the dentist came in and apologized for being late. He poked around in my mouth, said he had to do some laser treatment on my gums because I have "short teeth," and announced this procedure would be done in another room. Some guy came in and told me I had to sign the estimate for the procedure, assuring me that the $3,500 bucks was the price before the 15% discount. I was moved to the main room and waited another hour while techs did impression after impression of the tooth with no success. At this point, I was increasingly stressed over a gum-laser situation that was going to happen any second and yet never seemed to get started. They came back with another discount for my trouble. The estimator guy returned ten minutes later to report that Dr. Lynch was still with another patient, which he let me know was really my fault because they had to fit me in. No sir, three weeks before an appointment is not fitting anyone in. With that, I told them my relationship with the practice was concluded and asked that they take all the drool gear off my body. I walked out without looking back. I've now found the new dental love of my life, and like Dr. V, she treats me like her favorite and only patient.

I thought deeply about this experience in relation to my own business values. This new dentist, while undoubtedly skilled, failed to factor in the vulnerability of his patient. He functioned as a high-priced mechanic, not a caregiver. What could have made that experience tolerable, financially and otherwise? Empathy. Simple empathy. If "Not-Dr. V" had even bothered to say, "Lisa, wow, I bet this isn't what you want to be doing today, but we really care about making sure we get you the best treatment plan. It's a big investment of time, and it's expensive, but this is a true long-term solution for you. We've got a lot going on in the practice today, but we're going to move you as quickly as we can. Can we grab you something to read, or would you like your headphones to listen to music or a podcast?" A one-minute exchange with him could have transformed my experience. After I cut and run, I didn't even get a phone call back. Relationships are the centerpiece of service, which is something Flocksters understand. The new dentist might have been a genius in my mouth, but he lost the invitation to be there.

At Flock, we strive to create an experience that is everything that dental trip was not. I wanted a company built on compassionate empathy and teamwork, one that puts our shared needs before our individual ones. Since the beginning, I have maintained a commitment to being there for our stakeholders, whether they are clients, Flocksters, community partners, or the person at my side during my earliest days of landladying.

One of the losses I truly mourned when I was still in Arizona was Mike A's departure from the state after he took a job at the University of Southern California. That same Mike A, who showed me how to confidently transform Rubio into a home of my own with a lot of elbow grease, good friendships, and some basic supplies—some of which could be sourced from an alleyway or second hand store. We stayed in touch as our lives progressed, a dozen plus years of friendship having passed. I elected to move my change efforts from the world of nonprofits to the promising freedom a "for-profit" business presented. Mike earned his MBA, got married, got divorced, and when the time came for me to marry my spouse in 2009, Mike stood with me. Then, as people do, we drifted apart. Facebook offered a little glimpse here and there, and ten years (almost to the day) after my wedding, I got the urge to text him and see if he wanted to come work for my company. I truly do not know what inspired me at that moment. But Mike responded instantly that, in fact, it sounded good to him. About two months later, he was on payroll and nesting back into my world. Something had told me he needed a monumental life change, and I had built a company intended to offer just that to people.

Flock is designed to be a life-changing opportunity. It's a tall order for a little management company, but it's precisely what I want to do for people. How do you measure the impact and profitability of this gesture, the acceptance of that gesture, and what has come since? The reward is actually immeasurable. It feeds my soul to know I've built something that can be both a lifeline and life-changing. And having Mike back in my life is in some ways a return to my origin story and an opportunity to craft the next chapter of this business we're building.

When you have an empathy-based business, when your aim isn't only to make a profit for yourself but to make things better for the people around you, your community, and your planet, this kind of experience is less uncommon than you might think. When you place people above profits, the entire workplace paradigm shifts toward justice. And that's more profitable for everyone involved.

This is not without its downsides. When your coworkers are like family, their departures can feel like kids heading off to college and leaving behind an empty nest. One of the toughest departures I ever had to weather was that of Laura Van De Geijn. Laura was the first Nest employee. After a 20-minute phone interview, Jim and I were so impressed, we asked each other how many minutes we could wait before calling her back without looking desperate. We decided we didn't really care if we looked desperate. Three hours later, she arrived at our make-shift office, where we had dogs at our feet and needs that were growing by the minute. We knew when she hit the keyboard at 110 words a minute, she was meant to be. Her part-time job lasted two weeks, and Laura became full-time and absolutely essential in her first month.

There are few people who walk into your life and you know right away that they need to stay forever. Laura is one of those people for me and, frankly, for the entire Flock family. She worked to build a company that values employees as much as we do new business. She understood in her bones that the elegant intersection between growing our business and honoring our staff truly is a core value in our service-based business. When she decided to pursue her

MBA, I wrote in the next edition of the FlockLetter: "We're sad when she leaves for lunch! She's been the glue that holds us together, the brains behind the operation, and the calm during the storm."

Of course, I closed that piece with the hope that once Laura was armed with the skills and experience that an MBA offers, she would come back to join us for the next iteration of (what was then) Nest DC. Seven years have passed since Laura left. Two have passed since she came back, and our very first employee now holds the title of Vice President, Growth. Laura's return is one of my proudest testaments to having built the right team.

CHAPTER 12

THE CULTURE OF SECURITY: DON'T BE AFRAID TO BE AFRAID

When the pandemic hit, I worried hard. How would I protect my employees? How would I serve and soothe our clients and residents? Like every other nimble business, we moved online and began running board meetings via Zoom, leading virtual home inspections, offering camera-based maintenance diagnostics, and leveraging technology with vendors. We streamlined communications and found new efficiencies in our workflows that impacted everything from banking to processing applications and managing relationships. Most importantly, we were dogged about checking in and contributing to the wellness of our community, our residents, and our clients.

The onset of COVID required that we lean into our principle of optimizing operations, which meant we chose to risk making tough decisions too early, rather than bad decisions too late. In early March of 2020, long before any states began to issue stay-at-home directives, we furloughed our maintenance team, while projecting a $225,000 monthly drop in revenues. This resulted in not so much a financial gap to bridge, as much as a yawning, terrifying chasm. But there was no question: We needed to prioritize public health over profit and even solvency. I knew that working quickly to solve for the worst possible scenario would help us save our Flock in the long run.

As every good leader knows, the buck stops at the top. What every good leader also knows is that when the bucks run out, the top should be paid last. Tragically, this ethic is practiced so infrequently in the US that it has become an exception to celebrate and the rarest demonstration of servant leadership. Owners paying themselves last should be the rule, not the exception. I am the person who hired our teammates; they and their families rely on me for their livelihood. How could I have accepted a full paycheck during that time? I took a 75% pay cut for the duration of the crisis, taking home just enough to cover the mortgage, utilities, food, and the babysitter, who, at the time, could no longer babysit. I asked our management team to accept a five percent cut; in response, they offered ten. They also offered to halt their retirement savings payments, so the company could save on our 401k match program. We were running on fumes, operating in short-term crisis mode, and our leadership team was repeatedly demon-strating just why they had that designation.

Sadly, the behavior of some of my competitors reinforced why Flock is such an industry outlier. I witnessed landlords emailing impersonal newsletters screeching CORONAVIRUS in the subject line or, worse, nastygrams reminding tenants their rent was due on the first, no matter what. The more thoughtful property managers would, in strikingly insensitive language, inform their customers about the availability of public assistance and food banks.

At Flock, we refurbished our website to be a pandemic information hub. We sent residents newsletters infused with care, empathy, and positivity. Most importantly, we reduced rent by 15% in the buildings/units we own. A colleague asked why I did this. "What's the long game here? What was the strategy?" I didn't have a ready answer at the time, but I did it because I could. I did it because empathy is my engine. Let me assure you, I am no saint or martyr. I was in survival mode like everyone else, but for me, servant leadership is what helps me survive. The adrenaline rush I get when I'm trying to solve a big problem is like an opiate for me. Yet it's also a way of healing. Because my young life was marked by a deficit of concern for my state of mind and physical well-being, I developed a hunger for empathy. Since I wasn't get-ting the empathy I needed, I discovered as I grew up that showing empathy to others filled that void. This empathic urge, combined with a brazen need to be in charge, led me to stumble organically into a leadership style that I've refined over the years and which I've come to see as essential to the success of my business.

Empathy is not a common keyword in the property management industry or in business in general. I've been openly critical about my industry's lack of empathy or justice. Common perception suggests that in order to succeed, a landlord must resist all her empathic urges or simply fail. Flock has repeatedly shown this is not the case. Expressing empathy—in words and action—is what feeds me. I wish more people would try it. I wish our culture allowed for it. Some people have no idea how good it feels.

The same grit I used as a young side hustler served me well as the pandemic set in and continues to serve me well now. Ever since the backyard tool shed office, I've known that any company I started would be anchored in generosity. To that end, I've always measured profit not in mere dollars, but in the number of good jobs we create. Those good jobs mean people can do more than just pay their bills; they can also enjoy their lives and plan for a brighter future. I want to create career paths and provide healthcare and ensure people have time with their families, both now and always. So even when faced with an imminent and dramatic loss of revenue, the math is always simple: Profitability means good jobs, so we'd remain profitable as long as we could. The hardest moment I've ever experienced in any job anywhere came when I had to tell my employees that we needed to be worried for our livelihoods. I told them the leadership team was working on continuity, and I shared our short-term planning in great detail. I told them I was thinking of them 24/7. I was alone in my home office, saying these impossible, unthinkable words and knowing in my heart of hearts that, despite these dark circumstances, this was also one of the greatest moments of my professional life. I was occupying the intersection of concern, ingenuity, and innovation; panic, anxiety, and adrenaline; exhaustion, uncertainty, and grief; and sophisticated planning. At that moment, I was my very best self, professionally and personally. As a parent, as a boss, as a friend, as a citizen.

Making sacrifices for the team wasn't an exception, it was the expectation—all the way down to those years I went without a salary at all—because I'd promised to take care of my staff. And I did. As a kid, I wasn't always taken care of in the ways I needed to be. After my parents split, we kids were a bit under the radar to say the least. Over the summers, we toggled between our grandparents' houses. Both of my maternal grandparents were factory workers and retired from the Navy. They burned off steam at the American Legion while I occupied myself playing pool, drinking Shirley Temples, and avoiding handsy men. It was with my father's parents where I felt the most looked after and cared for. Their ranch had a retired American Quarter Horse. When I wasn't visiting, he got to do what he wanted—namely hang out with my grandmother and eat carrots. Grandma Sue was indulgent with me as well, though. My treat was having her saddle him up and point us both toward the Rocky Mountains. He grudgingly complied but dragged his feet—at least metaphorically. He tried to be patient, waiting for the return trip, and on my long-awaited command, we would fly home for more carrots and the ease of his pasture. I wanted him to be my best friend. His name—and I kid you not—was Mortgage. I wish I knew why. It was just one of those wild coincidences. We called him Morgie.

The farm was a loving embrace for me growing up. Nothing came close to the safety and comfort I enjoyed there. My grandmother died, and my aunt sent a thank you note I wrote to them, where I said I appreciated the food. And the air conditioning. And the bed. However lovely my grandmother was (and she *was*), the bar was pretty low if I was writing to thank folks for food and bedding during my summer "vacation."

"Grandma and Grappa. Thank you for havin me. And for food. And the air conditioning. And for the television and the bed." That's a pretty low bar for a kiddo on vacation. But all I needed was Grandma Sue. The love I got from her was never matched anywhere else in my youth, and she was the sole adult to consistently offer me empathy. "Consistently" is the operative term here. My mother's mental illness contributed to me feeling largely untethered and, sadly, uncared for. Unsafe. It meant that she couldn't or wouldn't always protect me from obvious danger and may explain why I care so much about tending to others. In her best moments, my mother was emotionally available to me in a way my father never was. She would tell me I could be president one day, even though I was sort of flunking out of school and hadn't mastered much beyond making money and playing the French horn. She wanted me to feel like anything was possible. I had to piece together what that meant, but I believed her.

It was during my youth that I discovered I was the person I could most rely on. I've been self-electing to not just take care of myself but to take care of those around me ever since.

It's why I was always clear that I had to stand up for and protect my staff, that I had to increase their ranks, their resources and their pay. You can't run a service-based business with servers that are underpaid and too few. The math was basic (the only kind I'm good at), even if the financial responsibilities scared me. Fortunately, the math worked, as did the team. And they worked hard. As the company thrived, I committed to bonusing nearly all profits back to the talent. We increased benefits whenever and however we could, adding cell phone coverage, commuter stipends, three-month paid family leave, profit-sharing, and more to our unlimited time off, fully paid healthcare, short- and long-term disability, 401k matches of 5%, and student loan assistance. We share the bounty, so much so that operating a "best place to work" sometimes felt like an exercise in outbidding ourselves. That's not to say that there wasn't the occasional employee who took these measures for granted, rather than understanding them as an investment in our culture and our team. In the minds of a few, no matter how much we did, it never seemed quite enough. Those were people who ultimately realized (or were told) that they weren't the best fit for our Nest. Most, however, were willing to give their all for a company that gave its all to them.

Before we reached the point of being able to offer an exceptional set of benefits, as we leaned on that cheap, young talent, I had to evaluate quickly what I could uniquely offer. I decided on a benefits package that honored the complex, 24/7 nature of the work but also didn't draw on resources. So we began with unlimited time off and flexible work hours. And we focused on culture all day long. Our casual office environment and laid back dynamic was born in those early days. We went to lunch as a team every Friday. First, it was pizza up the street, and later, we shifted to Pho Fridays at the Vietnamese restaurant across the street. We built community this way. It drew us together to share our love of the chaos and drama of the work. As a team, we were aligned for the clients we loved and against the bullies that began emerging early in the work. We suffered together through terrible hires. This included one maintenance employee who reorganized the materials in the van by shape and color. Another tech, one of our most experienced and skilled, was declared dead (and later upgraded to missing) when we tried to track him down with family. He had been injured at a Memorial Day picnic, had driven himself (in the company truck) to the hospital, and was MIA for a few days. Of course, we were worried about him. We also felt pretty shortsighted when we realized the keys to all the units were in that center truck console. Throughout it all, we have cultivated a sense of humor and a sense of family within our family of companies.

Before we could offer benefits that required cash outlays, we paired flexible schedules with the non-stuffy Silicon Valley vibe that was ubiquitous on the "Left Coast" but a true anomaly on the East Coast, especially at the time. DC is a company town, and that company is the federal government. While it may be host to more Democrats per capita than any place in the country, it's a conservative spot in many ways. Think no white after Labor Day and fashion trends for men that only include khaki, blue, and black. Back when I was doing a lot of fundraising in my nonprofit days, I often found myself on a train between NY and DC. As the trains inched closer to Manhattan's Penn Station, the passengers would become more colorful, the cuts of their clothing became more interesting, and their accessories expanded beyond ties and brooches. Then I'd head back to the District, where khakis and (rumpled) power suits reigned supreme. We might not have been able to pay big bucks, but we could liberate our team from DC's (lack of) fashion. So we didn't bother to dress up. It's much easier to cut and install tile without a pencil skirt anyway. (Plus, I haven't owned any kind of skirt since 1999.) Our offices were playful with bright colors, dogs at our feet, and music. We not only decorated our space for Halloween, but we also dressed our quail logo up as a witch, too. Why not? This was part of our differentiation, not only as a management company, but as an employer and a truly one-of-a-kind business.

Hiring the right people, as important as it is, can only get you so far if you're not willing to use your growing profits to create good jobs that come with good benefits. As someone committed to doing business differently, my top priority from our earliest days was to move from passable wages to competitive ones and to make sure everyone on staff had healthcare. Offering health coverage in a pre-Obamacare climate was likely one of the riskier things we did as a company from an investment perspective, but at no point did I think it wasn't the right thing to do. Luckily, as we were starting out, most of our team members were young and less expensive to insure. I also understood that some Flocksters—particularly those responding to maintenance requests and working with their hands—had a different relationship to healthcare. For me, this meant fully paid healthcare; short- and long-term disability insurance had to be a fundamental part of our early employment package. It was important that we not forget just how many people can't "pivot" their careers when their professional value is tied to skilled trades. When the industry or their bodies fail, options plummet quickly.

This theory of mine was tested when one of our most valued and valuable team members broke his wrist. This wasn't a simple sprain but a complex fracture that required surgery, rehab, and rest. With that single accident, he had to go on what seemed like indefinite leave. His absence was a substantial challenge to our workflows (and cash flows). Adding him as our in-house plumber was a game-changer when we made the investment, but the about face when he couldn't be scheduled was almost harder than taking the plunge (ahem) in the first place. In a single moment, his plans and ours were deeply disrupted. But we opted to look at his injury as an opportunity to shift gears and outsource work. His options would have been extremely limited had it not been for the short- and then long-term disability insurance he leaned on. Those company-paid policies got him through what wound up being nearly a year of healing. This modest investment in insurance we made, plus patience and team members willing to fill gaps, allowed us to keep his job open for him during that time. Ironically or not, this was a team member who'd been skeptical of every benefit we offered, from our 401k and educational savings plans to our insurance. This was, in part, because they required setting up a traditional bank account. I can now say with confidence that we were able to eclipse that trust delta. At Flock, we have not only invested in benefits that are aligned with our values, but we've operated with those values as well.

THE DIVERSITY + THE ALLY ADVANTAGE

Our culture is about far more than generous benefits and enjoying each other's company. It is also very much about our core values, all rooted in justice. One of those core values is to consider differences the norm and see diversity and allyship as part of our identity, not a corporate checkbox. My business instincts are backed by science and nicely outlined in the Coleman Report, a landmark study on education and equality in the 1960s.[39] Although the Congressionally-funded study was expected to reveal patterns of racial inequality and segregation in schools, Coleman unearthed an even more pronounced predictor of academic success for children: socioeconomic diversity among students. While exposure to a breadth of experiences clearly benefits us as children, it's an easy bet that the advantage doesn't end when we cross the threshold of adulthood. I can't help subscribing to the idea that homogeneity in a workplace is counterproductive to sustainability, growth potential, organizational culture, and more. That's why we work to attract top talent from a variety of backgrounds, whether socioeconomic, racial, geographic, or

---

[39] Kahlenberg, "Why Did It Take So Long for Class-Based School Integration to Take Hold?"

other. Top talent can't be confused with degrees from top schools or the exclusivity of pedigree. I don't have either, and my grit and discipline have been the credentials I needed the most on this journey.

Diversity, inclusion, pathways to equity—these have to be baked into the corporate mix rather than something to check off a list. Furthermore, if a business's intention is to serve a community, it should create jobs supporting people who represent the breadth of that community. There is no downside to this value system. It helps us learn. The Coleman report found that "[the] educational resources provided by a child's fellow students are more important for his achievement than are the resources provided by the school board."[40] Why would we expect the workplace to be any different? At Flock, we believe creating an environment that will allow everyone to soar is our responsibility. And it bothers me deeply that as a woman, a mother, a member of the LGBTQ community, and a product of an insecure household, I am not afforded the same opportunities that are abundant for those with means, those who were born at the right time and place to people that fit neatly into that homogenous framework and are sadly hardwired to privilege. Let's start remapping these cultural and corporate models of privilege because they are built on models of scarcity. And scarcity puts any hope of a collectively bright future at risk.

---

[40] Kahlenberg, "Why Did It Take So Long for Class-Based School Integration to Take Hold?"

In the end, the culture we have at Flock is reflective of the kind of environment I want to work in. My previous jobs far too often failed to foster a sense of community or even respect. Early in my nonprofit career, and even in my days as a graduate student, I was struck (and almost struck down) by a kind of hazing I experienced. This hazing wasn't even aimed to be a rite of passage or create experiences that would bind participants together for life. It was purely antagonistic and often came from women leaders who chose to actively undermine other women in their sphere, instead of providing mentorship and support. Given that, on first pass, I'd chosen a career in women's health and public policy that supported women's rights, the opportunities for disappointment were plentiful. I later made a shift to the environmental sector, where I found the intergenerational toxicity to be even more pronounced and dangerous.

Despite having been in senior management positions in organizations focused on social good, I began to see that the only way to enjoy a thriving workplace that reflected my values was to create my own. All the disappointing work experience I had prior to Flock gave me a chance to pocket ideas for a workplace of my own—one that could shed those problematic trends and give people a true opportunity to advance and blossom professionally. I never dreamed I would make this workplace culture a reality for 70 human beings. Yet, I can say with almost total confidence that I've created a feminist fortress that advances and supports the success of women. In it, we flourish without the toxicity of women hating women, and we enjoy the respect and collaboration between all genders that gives me hope for a much more equal future. At Flock, we have created a culture that I am proud of and one I want to inspire others to advance.

THE MOTHERHOOD ADVANTAGE

I was a hesitant parent. It's no wonder, given much of the origin story that I've shared here. Parenthood has been, for me, just as expected. There is an intensity of love and hard work. It's life-changing, and the weight of parenthood and its responsibilities are like no other I have experienced in my life-time. It's also a risk. Will this human share my values? Will he, too, have the justice lens that I so deeply value? Will he take his privilege for granted? How does one protect and provide without creating entitlement? As I write this, our son is just shy of double digits. He is a thoughtful and kind boy. I not only love but deeply admire him. He is gentle and emotional and a product of his environment—by design. He recently pondered aloud why the gas station where we get our cars fixed had such tricky hours. "What is she thinking!?!" he exclaimed.

"What do you mean, bud?"

"The woman who owns that gas station must give up a lot of business by not being open on a Saturday." It didn't occur to that kid for a moment that a man might own the station. So, it's no surprise that he asks other kids what their moms do for a living. He is watching, listening, and learning the values we are living. I'm grateful for that. And I now see parenthood was a risk worth taking. But there wasn't really any modeling for me to believe parenthood was compatible with my drive or commitment to justice for all vs. justice for my own little family.

What's common among moms is this sense of compromise we'll face when growing our families. The calculus is challenging. Will our careers stall? Will the lift of motherhood diminish our ability to perform? Will opportunities fade into the background because women are seen as less valuable and therefore valued less once we have children? The answer is obviously a resounding yes. Women are quite simply, more likely to see their careers stall, slow, or cease when they elect to become parents. Of course, we know balancing family and career isn't a matter of choice, but we shouldn't have to choose one over the other as a matter of gender destiny. That certainly wasn't going to be my path. And damned if I would let it be the path for my fellow colleagues who are also part of the parenting journey.

As the owner of a business, I have substantially more agency around what kind of life and future I pursue for myself, my family, and, importantly, my team members. Earlier this year, Grace announced cheerfully that it might be nice to have a socially-distanced, last-minute, in-person meeting after a Zoom check in. The tedium of pandemic collaboration was weighing heavily on me, so I understood her interest. But it was out of character for her. She had a lot on her plate without a last-minute drive to my house to sit in the cold and catch up. It wasn't possible that day, so with a bit of hesitation and a lot of joy, she shared with me, via the glow of my monitor, news that she was pregnant. Having children had always been in the cards for Grace, and we had discussed her future as a mom often. But her timing surprised me. She had postponed a wedding and, with the rest of us, openly pondered how the pandemic would further impact her life's future. She and her partner chose to follow their dreams sooner than later because life will never be certain, and there is no reason to stop living it. I was so proud of this brave decision and investment in the future.

A few months later, a second (and the second most senior) team member shared news she and her wife were also expecting—just weeks after Grace was to deliver her own son. I knew Steph was nervous telling me, just like Grace had been. I knew both were asking the same questions I was when deciding to begin a family. With the luxury of hindsight and nine parent years under my belt, I could offer each of them a salve for their unspoken concerns.

As leaders, as women, as a company, we have to scoot over and make room for families. We have the benefit of flexibility and the startup advantage that allows us to be as creative as we need to be. My commitment to work and building a company certainly changed when our son arrived. There was more to navigate and a steeper hill to climb as a woman. But I had an entirely different kind of motivation and drive once Beckett joined our family. I wanted to model hard work and justice at once while creating a safe, secure environment for our child to thrive. I needed to find creative ways to be present for him and for my family. But I also needed to be present and inspirational for our family of team members. I had to focus on what I do best and learn to delegate. I had to trust my talent and grow them quickly. I'm quite certain our Flock has been successful, not despite my role as a mom but, in large part, because of it. As I shared this story of my own start in the world as a mom and businesswoman, Steph responded with a raised eyebrow, clearly surprised that I credited much of my "corporate" success to motherhood, rather than blaming it for a stalled career or one that made me so deeply exhausted, I couldn't enjoy any part of my life, kiddo included. I was lucky to have so much agency. In an ideal work world, abundance and agency are foundational.

In her book *Radical Candor*, Kim Scott reminds us that just like companies evolve, so does their talent. "We are not fixed assets in a corporate setting. Life changes. Sometimes we're superstars; sometimes we're rockstars. Sometimes we're the nimble, flexible people who are able to go all in. Sometimes we have to downshift to be present for what is new in life— like a child, or an illness, or personal drive to seek something other than corporate success. These natural transitions in life shouldn't be seen as a hindrance to success but as a chance to create environments for whole beings. Rather than deploying talent as an asset, we think of talent as our identity—and identities are mutable. Without embracing change and seeing it as an inevitable path to growth, we'll be short-changing ourselves and the team members ready to double down on career while others pace set for a minute." (50).[41]

As a function of servant leadership, creating space for parenthood, for full personhood, is essential. We can't expect our talent to serve our clients, our residents, or our community if we don't serve them. This is just business—and just capitalism.

---

[41] Scott, *Radical Candor*, 74.

PART SIX

CHAPTER 13

ABUNDANCE
IN PRACTICE

Having read this far, you've likely picked up on how important it is for us at Flock to walk the talk. That's partly because walking the talk is really just a simpler way of saying we anchor ourselves in our purpose and values. It's the path of justice. And "anchor" is an important term. Anchors keep us grounded and steady our location. They should also provide us with a sense of security, of comfort. After all, they keep us from floating away from what matters. They should also invoke a sense of fearlessness. I've worked hard to build a team at Flock unafraid to use their creativity to provide best-in-class service to our clients and residents. And I haven't been afraid to make sure they reap the rewards of those efforts. That's one of the reasons profit sharing is an essential feature of our value system as a company.

There is a lot going on under "profit" in the Merriam Webster dictionary. Profit can be

"1. a valuable return: gain
2. the excess of returns over expenditure in a transaction or series of transactions
3. the compensation accruing to entrepreneurs for the assumption of risk in business enterprise as distinguished from wages or rent"

But my favorite, and what resonates with me the most, is the definition of profit as a transitive verb, "to be of service, to benefit."[42] Now let's study the benefactor and the beneficiary in a justice-driven company like Flock.

As someone who grew up without a lot of financial security, wealth creation has been a strong personal motivator for me as an entrepreneur. It has never, however, trumped the change I want to see—and be—in the world. With that in mind, I've used our profits as a valuable tool to live my values and reinvest in a business model that assumes an abundance, versus a scarcity approach to managing resources. In other words, there will be more profits, so there is no need to hoard the cash. In fact, it's a better investment to share those profits with the people who helped you generate them. From our first years as a company, sharing in the losses and the wins was non-negotiable. There was something deeply unsettling to me about the assumption that after I paid the bills and

---

[42]Merriam Webster, "profit."

made payroll, whatever was left at the end of the day would be mine. I could bet the farm, buy the bigger house or condo. None of that pleased me. I was quick to realize that what did please me was rewarding the team that actually delivered those profits. Without them, I couldn't have a viable business, let alone a profitable one. By reinvesting those profits where they originated—with the talent—I bet on my team, believing that would pay richer dividends than keeping all the cash for myself. Who wants to be the jerk at the table who eats the whole appetizer? For me, the polite thing to do is share. That includes significant company profits.

In all honesty, profit sharing produces meaningful outcomes for your business and yourself. If anything, it's just wealth postponed or reimagined. Profit sharing lowers costs and protects against disruptive staff turnover. It gives staff more financial security and the ability to thrive. Worrying about money all the time while trying to make ends meet doesn't inspire focused, hard work or innovative contributions. It's a distracting, anxiety-producing, and painful state of being that I don't want my team to suffer through. Profit sharing invites people into the world of opportunity that comes from having more resources. Profit sharing can be the difference between renting and owning for a team member. It can offer the financial means to follow dreams, like traveling to far-off places or adding to your family, and it can deliver staff from the burdens of crushing student loan debt or struggling to care for family members in need. Over the years, we've shared just under one million dollars in company profits with Flocksters. Sometimes—well, most of the time—it meant a bank account at the end of the year that was so empty it echoed when we checked the "balance." It meant a willingness on my part to forgo additional compensation or borrow from the future to give back to team members today. This is how a just business can function as a profit magnet and not a downshift in success.

The pure joy and sense of satisfaction I get from sharing my (material) success is substantial, but it's not always a sweetheart story. This model has to be embedded in the culture, so that profit sharing doesn't become an entitlement. Profit sharing also can't be used to justify poor compensation the rest of the year. To work, it has to be above and beyond fair-to-generous wages and benefits. And while I am a fierce advocate for and passionate defender of a profit sharing model, there are, without a doubt, times when the model falls flat, like when team members fail to appreciate the windfalls or become disconnected from the meaning and only focus on their own unique interests.

When profit sharing failed to land as intended in my company, it hurt. During a quarterly retreat with a clutch of new Flocksters, we played a round of company Jeopardy® to see who had a handle on our history, culture, and core values. In a year when we had shared close to $300,000 in profits, the average guess about how much we'd reinvested in staff was in the 20s. I wanted to cry. It became immediately apparent to me that we couldn't live our values unless we're talking about them, operationalizing them, and honoring them. We had to be transparent about what makes our company so exceptional. And being exceptional wasn't a top down proposition.

If we couldn't sell ourselves to ourselves, what were we selling to our customers? If staff couldn't understand the magnitude of the investments we were making in them and the values behind them, our leadership was failing to create a shared understanding of what made our corporate, justice-driven approach not only impactful, but also really special.

Practically speaking, profit sharing models can be as basic or as complex as you would like them to be. We codified ours for transparency and accountability. We committed to our staff, in writing, that we would designate profit allocations accordingly: 40% in cash investments to staff, 30% to reserves, and 30% toward building company capacity with staff input on those priorities. We invested in technology, space, tools, vehicles, marketing, community contributions, and, most importantly, staffing that allowed for growth and position right-sizing. We didn't want a company dependent on burning people out or a staff model that was overly dependent on certain individuals working constantly. Truly, every dollar in profit was used to create a better, more productive workplace, and the expectation was that our profit sharing would lead to stronger growth, better service, and a healthy culture. We more or less nailed it at the philosophical and cultural level, but we still have to continuously rethink how we deliver on our profit-sharing promise. Is it negotiable? Is the money evenly distributed? Are there performance expectations for eligibility? Or is it a mutable, evolving process? Different companies have to answer these questions for themselves because what works in one setting may be disastrous in another, especially in contexts where the business landscape can change on a dime. We all lived that reality in 2020. Being nimble and working within a lean startup model leaves room for a highly responsive approach to profit sharing.

Perhaps most importantly, a profit-sharing model gives teams a real-time return on their contribution to Flock's growth and success. When *we* do better, *they* do better. It's a simple calculation, and when we're growing and thriving as a company, our value and values as a company flourish. I'm asked often why I give away all the money (because I don't include myself in profit sharing rounds). People pose this question as if I'm making some kind of sacrifice. But Flock is like a tree. It's fine to share the fruits and gather in the abundance of shade the tree delivers. In the end, though, no matter how I distribute the fruits, the tree itself is mine to do with as I wish. I intend, with this book, to see orchards emerging in the business world, breathing new life into selfish and outdated corporate models that separate the haves and have nots and that fail to work in service of a better, highly oxygenated world.

I've always loved wandering neighborhoods. The best time is at night, wondering how life is unfolding for a fellow home-dweller, whether they are happy or worried, content or struggling. This is a time to clear my head, walk a dog, or connect with a friend. That time on my feet is an invitation for reflection and restoration.

During the early years of my son's life, I would find space for those walks whenever I could. I snuck those moments in while he napped or got ready for bed with his other mom. Even 20 minutes gave me a chance to catch up with an old friend or think about past moments or what was coming up. One early evening, I was deep in conversation with my best friend, Frances. With my two shelter dogs, I spotted a bright white dove tucked under a bush looking both scared and sweet. Instinctively and without skipping a beat, I bent down and gently picked this dove up, as if I had done so a million times. I suppose I had. This dove was like an old family friend, looking identical to one I wandered home with in the 5th grade (much to mother's initial dismay). I called him Romeo and immediately wondered how long this vocal but beautiful being would be sharing a room with me. My parents, brother, and I were all living in close quarters. (As I mentioned earlier in the book, mine was the only legal bedroom in the house.) While I knew dogs lived for years, I assumed this bird would meet a near-term end like my hermit crabs and the various rodents we hosted as kids. But Romeo wouldn't have a dramatic ending anytime soon. In fact, that bird lived until I was in graduate school, my mom's true pride and joy. And even then, his ending was premature.

As I turned my hand to look this newest runaway dove square in the eyes, I told my friend Frances by bluetooth, "Woah, I just picked this dove up on the side of Piney Branch Road."

"Huh," she said, "I hope you like your new dove."

Maybe she should have been the one to own and operate the Sherlock Holmes Detective Agency because she could see the future. This dove had found its forever home and would, soon enough, become iconic in its own right. That twenty-minute walk between bath and bedtime had taken a turn. I hustled to situate my feathered old friend in a cat carrier, certain I would jump on the neighborhood Listservs and help this dove land back home. Surely this bird was tame and had a family. I named her Juliette, of course. But days and weeks went by without a family emerging to claim her. The cat carrier quickly became a small birdcage, which soon became a full, free-standing enclosure I imposed on the office and staff while we "waited to see what happened." Eventually, I learned the dove was lost during a magic show (or perhaps was an escapee?). The magician turned out to have a record for inappropriate behavior with children and only bothered to check on the bird when there was a show coming up. There was no way my dove was going to be used as child bait. With that, I ordered a custom made, mid-century modern wood cage for wing stretching and perching in between indoor, free-range flight time. The magician told me the bird was a boy, and since I was learning Spanish, I renamed him Julio. Love is love, and Romeo and Julio would also make a lovely pairing. Later, when Julio laid eggs, we switched to something noncommittal: Julietto. It was perfect. She and I commuted, with the dogs, back and forth to work each day. She made the journey in a bag from Sweetgreen with a custom window.

Later, in what seemed to be the worst of the pandemic, I began letting Julietto enjoy time in the backyard under my watchful eye. And on one of those days, she flew high into a tree monitored by a neighbor cat. My eyes wandered, and she took her best last flight as she thought to join the cat on the same branch. R.I.P., sweet girl. Peacekeeper until the end.

Six months later, I found myself walking along a dark road near the big pond in Edgewater, Maryland, where we have a second home among 70s tract houses and an incredible habitat for birds. Together with the bald eagles, oracles, herons, osprey, and blue jays, I feel plenty (socially) distant. But not in an entirely bad way. One night, I headed out for a walk but chose not to share the time with a friend. I was deep in thought, wondering what would become of the companies if something happened to me. It was one of those morbid, but necessary, conversations any of us should have as business owners and as parents—particularly during a pandemic. What kind of legacy did I want to leave behind? To whom would I pass along my abundance, and why?

Honestly, I've always had the answer to this question. I just hadn't been resourced enough to answer it. It was on the tip of my tongue every time my family packed up for another apartment, another town, another opportunity. It was even there simmering in the background when I sold cousin Richard's Civic for $8,300. It was the writing on the wall when I spread seed for the backyard doves on Rubio Avenue. I wanted others to enjoy the freedom and the security and the value of home ownership. I dreamed of helping others buy those homes. And I was pretty sure, as I rounded the corner on that walk, I didn't need to be dead to follow that dream.

Jeff Hoffman, the global entrepreneur who is also a best-selling author and award-winning producer, among other skills, has said, "You may be successful, but will you matter?

Success is doing for yourself. Mattering is doing something for someone else. Your success is someone else's miracle."[43] Hoffman's proclamation is about action today—not the arm-chair activity of someone resting their case on yesterday's success. Legacy implies past tense, but I am interested in changing lives now—and quickly. Our success is someone else's miracle, and the idea and application of birdSEED creates a critical path toward reparative justice.

PAY IT BACKWARDS

birdSEED is my (and Flock's) real-time legacy and an impressive counterpoint to the toxic, deliberately racist history of real estate and the industries that have supported it. With birdSEED, we can build pathways to increase intergenerational wealth, challenge racism, and advance a more just and equitable future. With this work, we found our voice and our moment to ask for something different from our industry. We were looking for something from property management beyond a moderate statement about Black Lives Matter and a company happy hour to support Habitat for Humanity—all delivered while benefiting from redlining, steering, predatory lending, and foreclosures. I shared this piece in the *Washington Post*, just after the January 6th insurrection and

---

[43] Kuchler, "The Power of People and Leaving a Legacy (by Jeff Hoffman)."

in the middle of a national conversation, if not reckoning, around race:[44]

> The real estate industry, property management included, has a history of toxic and racist practices that make up its origin story of profitability. Try as I might, it's impossible to divorce our success from this history. While we believe fundamentally that quality, dignified housing is a basic human right, this right is largely reserved—by design and policy—for white people.
>
> I could argue that this is not a past we (Flock) contributed to, but the reality is that my company continues to reap its benefits. This makes us responsible for working toward an equitable and racially just future in housing. Understanding the past is part and parcel of creating that equitable future.
>
> It seems like an uphill battle when *The Post* reports median home prices in D.C. are north of $1 million.[45] This is a data point celebrated by many homeowners awash in equity and spirit-crushing for those with dreams of ownership in DC. What's left for most is a rental market that too often has earned its bad reputation. The most alarming part? None of this happened by accident.
>
> Property owners and managers have played a starring role in discrimination in housing. Sadly, at times, housing

---

[44] Wise, "Opinion | Housing Justice Is a Basic Human Right."

[45] Lerner, "Report: Median Sales Price of Houses in D.C. Now Exceeds $1 Million."

policy has intentionally delivered, codified, and practiced systemic racism throughout the country. These trends have played out in the real estate sales market, and property management has contributed mightily to this injustice.

Intentionally restricted housing inventory has fed discriminatory practices in DC and beyond. Segregation suppressed the supply of decent housing for Black and brown residents. The industry's economics favored lowering the basic living standards for largely urban homes while increasing prices along the way.

White families were being repositioned in shiny new homes outside urban cores. Their tax dollars created thriving schools and neighborhoods that were more or less homogeneous by design. Segregation in real estate has been thriving along with the intergenerational advantage white landowners have enjoyed from the very beginning. Along with it, inequity, discrimination, and oppression also surge—but under the framework of policies that were, at least on paper, intended to achieve the opposite.

Think public housing, public-private housing partnerships and, under the Federal Housing Administration, the emergence of predatory inclusion,[46] which paired qualified Black mortgage applicants with substantially substandard housing or unfair loans. This rinse-and-repeat cycle generated a new and profitable foreclosure industry, and those homes were either resold or placed back into the rental market, where inventory was as low as the housing quality.

---

[46]Holtzman, "The Age of Predatory Inclusion."

Today, the story is similar. One-third of DC-owned public housing is nearly uninhabitable.[47] You have to wonder what details separate barely livable from uninhabitable. It's likely a matter of degree. And history isn't just repeating itself with public housing stock but in the private rental market as well.

Let's look at the affordable housing and voucher programs in DC. Residents with subsidies (housing vouchers) face explicit (and implicit) bias from an industry with active workarounds for property owners who don't want to comply with fair housing laws. These cheats include raising prices for listings over the market rate to avoid voucher applicants and using unrealistic credit scores minimums or rental history as screening criteria. Some openly turn away voucher applicants or use technology workarounds on their listings to "kick out" inquiring applicants with subsidized income, most of whom, in this region, are people of color. One new trend is to include a "subscription fee" for folks interested in merely seeing active rental listings from that company. Individuals with subsidies aren't typically positioned (or dumb enough) to pay a fee just to see possible listings. These practices are blatantly and dangerously discriminatory.

Simply banning property owners from discriminating against applicants with subsidies is not enough. Unfortunately, there are significant barriers and disincentives for

---

[47] Baskin, "DCHA Says Thousands of Units Are Nearly Uninhabitable. Tenants Want to Know: What's Next?"

those industry professionals interested in creating pathways for applicants with subsidies provided by governmental programs. Inspection hurdles, bureaucratic hoops, and extended timelines mean some owners with applicants waiting urgently for housing have units sit vacant for months and months while program compliance is being sought. This substantially slows the pace of the market for those in urgent need of essential, dignified housing. Even a missing street number can push availability timelines by months.

We're ready to break those patterns and envision a future where housing justice is a basic human right.

After we bet on equity with birdSEED, I needed to ensure the sustainability of the company that would indeed make a difference in the world. After, at last, tying our work to housing justice and sharing our profits by sharing ownership, the only way to outperform myself was to truly share the wealth. So my last will and testament leaves the controlling share of Flock to the Flock Leadership Team.

This decision came about very naturally because it leaned on my innate generosity. Since I have a bad habit of giving away a future I haven't quite visualized, succession planning has been a valuable reality check for me. If the true value of the Flock family of companies lies in the talent and leadership, it only makes sense that my succession planning must be rooted in the preservation of that team and the culture that supported it. If my intention was to build a company with staying power, then I needed to identify how that company could exist and continue to thrive and push my vision forward without my being there. As with Roost, ownership inspires an entirely different commitment and passion for the work. It's infused with opportunities that aren't given traditional salaried or hourly employees. Ownership comes with greater responsibility but also hope for a brighter future and more control over what that future might look like. By leaving Flock to the flock, I've ensured my legacy will always be gaining altitude. It can continue to feed my family and fund the work of the birdSEED foundation. The succession planning is layered, leaving my estate with 30% silent ownership. Whole- and term-life insurance policies will generate enough income to allow the leadership team to purchase the balance of the company from my estate, up to five million in value. After that, we've earmarked the value of the company to be allocated to birdSEED and to opportunities for future team members to experience ownership through a shareholder fund. (This is still very much being worked out as we go to print. I had no idea how complicated and nuanced this planning could be, but ultimately, it's a sign of true success that sorting out a future comes with infinite possibilities and complexity.) But legacy can have little impact without this planning.

I've discussed this plan with my wife more times than I can count. In most aspects of our lives, she's the boss, but with succession planning, she has followed my lead and always fully supported our gifting a large portion of the company back to the employees. The insurance makes that an easier decision, but she recognizes that retaining 30% ownership of companies that are purpose-driven and thriving is the best possible investment. The alternative is to focus on the simplicity of the financial transaction and see it as a paper investment, but that is not the kind of legacy I intend to leave behind.

My succession plan, like my leadership of Flock and much of my life, is also deeply rooted in the concept of abundance. If we choose to believe there is enough for everyone—and there is—the instinct to hoard and protect what we've hunted and gathered can relax. This brings to mind the famous 1972 marshmallow experiment.[48] The study intended to test willpower, impulse control, and delayed gratification in children. A child was put into a room with a marshmallow and told that if they could refrain from eating the marshmallow, they could have an additional one after a certain period of time passed. Social scientists wanted to assess delayed gratification as an indicator of future successes. They followed those marshmallow kids from the early 70s and determined that a child's capacity to delay gratification indeed signified their potential for success.

This study was recreated in the 1990s, however, and elicited an entirely different set of conclusions. As Jessica McCrory Calarco, an assistant professor of sociology at Indiana University, wrote in *The Atlantic*: "Ultimately, the new study finds limited support for the idea that being able to delay gratification leads to better outcomes. Instead, it suggests that the capacity to hold out for a second marshmallow is shaped in large part by a child's social and economic background—and,

---

[48]Clear, "40 Years of Stanford Research Found That People with This One Quality Are More Likely to Succeed."

in turn, that that background, not the ability to delay gratification, is what's behind kids' long-term success."[49]

The study illustrates the behavioral considerations that participants face in an environment marked by scarcity vs. abundance. If you're raised in a setting where you're unsure when the next marshmallow may present itself, holding out for a second is both counterintuitive and in conflict with your self-preservational instincts. For children raised in an environment of abundance, the multiplier isn't implausible, and patience begets predictable reward patterns. I've often observed how our son, Beckett, can wait days before indulging in a marshmallow—even without the promise of a second. (Fun fact: We buy him a donut every time we fly. And he waits until he's in his seat with the tray table down before he'll eat it, even if there is a six-hour delay). I've wondered whether this is a function of abundance or his own unique personality, and I think it's a blend of the two. But what I can say with absolute certainty is that my son never has been—and likely never will be—hungry as a result of scarcity. That privilege allows him a degree of safety that is reserved for the precious few who win the uterine lottery.

BE POLITICAL

When I elected myself to create the stability and security that my family had been unable to create for me, I simultaneously

---

[49]Calarco, "Why Rich Kids Are So Good at the Marshmallow Test."

elected myself to act on big ideas that would extend far beyond me. This involves being politically engaged. I'm not talking about writing big checks. If anything, my model is a counterpoint to those who use their big corporate check-books to meddle in politics by buying their way into the good graces of elected officials. That's not change making; it's self-preservation. At Flock, we're invested in an activist model for change. It's not simply about advocacy, but also about action. It's about creating jobs. It's about contributing to the com-munity financially and with our time and talent. It's not about surrounding ourselves with shareholders (the decision makers, elected officials, and other "haves"); it's about aligning with those affected by our work, with an audience of stakeholders. The good news is that a stakeholder and a shareholder can be one in the same. Apologies to Milton Friedman (not really), but an audience of only shareholders generates a corporate mandate that is only about financial metrics. Friedman's views, which he espoused in the 60s, have come to be known as the "Friedman Doctrine" and argues that the only responsibil-ity a company has is to increase the wealth of its investors.[50] Our company values don't line up with that traditional man-date. In fact, if they did, I believe we would be less profitable.

To be sure, I am not the only one espousing that busi-nesses abandon their values (if they exist) to put investor returns above all else. In 1984, Dr. R. Edward Freeman at the

---

[50]Friedman, "A Friedman Doctrine—The Social Responsibility Of Business Is to Increase Its Profits."

University of Virginia developed the stakeholder theory.[51] He argued that businesses actually have an array of stakeholders—including employees, the local community, vendors, suppliers, and more—that they need to consider. He also questioned the laughable idea that only people, not corporations, can have any responsibility. (I'm betting a whole slew of class-action attorneys would laugh out loud at that.) Even Harvard professors Joseph L. Bower and Lynn S. Paine argue that the Friedman Doctrine can stifle innovation and risk-taking.[52] It's not just professors who question a shareholder mentality, either. Jack Welch, chairman and CEO of General Electric for 20 years, called prioritizing shareholder value above all else, "the dumbest idea in the world."[53]

Focusing on stakeholders might be seen as partisan. That's okay. Any client who abandons us because we support Black Lives Matter or encouraged people to vote Trump out of office or hosted a vigil for the late Supreme Court Justice Ruth Bader Ginsburg is, well, a client who should be flying with a different flock.

If there has ever been a time for a company to play their political cards, now seems like a good one. Local and global unrest will continue to impact us all, and this moment in time

[51] "About the Stakeholder Theory."

[52] Bower, Paine, "The Error at the Heart of Corporate Leadership."

[53] Denning, "Making Sense Of Shareholder Value: 'The World's Dumbest Idea'."

has the potential to fundamentally change the trajectory of our economy and of humanity's capacity to live on this planet. While it may seem bizarre for a property management company to be justice-driven, it's equally curious that a spice company would emerge from left field, publicly loud and proud as a justice warrior.

You might not expect a company with fun product names like *Mural of Flavor* and *Arizona Dreaming* to be aggressive about anything, but during President Trump's impeachment trial and the Black Lives Matter protests of 2020, Penzeys Spices founder, Bill Penzey, stepped forward in a way that inspired me to be even more unapologetically political. Penzeys is America's largest independent spice retailer, with 53 stores around the country and headquarters just outside of Milwaukee, Wisconsin. Since its beginnings in the 1980s, Bill has been vocal politically and socially, writing opinion pieces for a column in their catalog, which was historically mailed to half a million customers. Penzeys branding is political activism and kindness. They trademarked the phrase "season liberally," and they hire staff who "believe that cooking is kindness and that kindness can change the world."

Fast forward to 2016. Bill had replaced the paper catalogs with an email newsletter called "Voice of Cooking," and had written a scathing letter to his followers criticizing President Trump and the Republican Party. In the letter he said, "The open embrace of racism is unleashing a wave of ugliness unseen in this country for decades," and he called on other business leaders to "stand up for the values of America."[54]

---

[54] Rosner, "The C.E.O. Who Called Trump a Racist."

He knew he would lose customers over this statement. In fact, he was prepared to lose 10% to 30% of sales, but he said he was "willing to take a hit for what was right." He did lose some customers when right-leaning groups declared a spice boycott, but he also gained new customers who were better aligned with his values. After that newsletter went out, Penzeys online sales increased by 60%—that's a lot of cinnamon and cayenne pepper!

Penzeys went even further in October 2019 when they purchased $700,000 worth of Facebook ads in support of Trump's impeachment. (The only other group that outspent them during that time period was Trump's campaign.)[55] This wasn't a hot-headed spending spree; this was part of a well-developed and intentional advertising strategy. They even had product promotions to match the activism with "Impeachment Day" offers. Remember that paper catalog they used to send out? When Penzeys stopped mailing catalogs, they made the decision to use those marketing dollars on social media ads with an outspoken political stance. He said he lost some of his "AM radio-listening" customers,[56] but finally made traction in gaining engagement with spice-loving millennials.

In 2020, Penzeys anti-racism position was on display after their Minneapolis store was damaged during a demonstration protesting the murder of George Floyd. In a statement that

[55] Mehta, "Mixing Politics and Parsley: Why This Spice Seller Spent $700,000-plus on Facebook Ads for Trump's Impeachment."

[56] Rosner, "The C.E.O. Who Called Trump a Racist."

he tweeted, Bill said, "If sweeping up some glass and replacing a couple of windows is a piece of everybody realizing the costs of racism-fueled police violence toward minorities is no longer affordable, so be it." And later that same year, when demonstrators took to the streets in Kenosha to protest the police shooting of Jacob Blake, Bill opened up their Kenosha shop and began giving away all of its contents, exemplifying for business owners more concerned about property damage than justice, "Human life means everything; stuff, not so much."[57]

My personal politics were well-established during my youth. Those early days in Hailey were marked by a contrast that seemed nearly impossible to reconcile, and I had a front row seat to two different narratives unfolding among my classmates. One girl I remember lived a handful of blocks from school, and she and her family appeared to be living in the kind of poverty where you always seem to get along, but it's scary, and there are a lot of creative solutions in play. Her family got most of their vegetables from what the local grocery store had tossed out as bad. She convinced me, as her family hosted me for meals now and then, that the produce was perfectly good. They weren't wrong, but the circumstances certainly were. Other evenings, when one super rich child or

---

[57] Reneau, "Penzey's Spices Is 'Looting' Its Own Kenosha Store in a Statement about Priorities."

another had to invite every classmate to a party, I would find myself at a fancy restaurant, closed for the guest of honor. Something in the middle had to be more just. Something between well-timed dumpster dives and middle schoolers being served mocktails with a live band playing and chocolate fountains in every corner. My appetite was for justice.

Somewhere in the mid-1970s, I called Pocatello, Idaho, my Idahome. Around the same time, my somewhere-in-her-mid-to-late-20s mother was a newly-minted divorcee and an enthusiastic ceramicist and printmaker. Together with a stained-glass artisan named Judy, she rented a gallery space in the (still) not thriving downtown. We'd pull up in her brown Pinto and proceed to shape some of my fondest memories. With me by her side, Mom would throw pots, spinning one piece after another. We'd stuff the kiln full of art that paired well with macramé, from bud vases to ash trays, waiting eagerly to see what emerged more beautiful from the boxed inferno. I loved everything about it. It was tactile, practical, and involved a cash register.

That was the same decade when Ruth Bader Ginsburg rose up as a legal powerhouse in her volunteer role with the ACLU. In the latter part of the 70s, I vividly remember riding my bike through the streets of Hailey, Idaho, drumming up votes (or not, in this case) for President Jimmy Carter. He might not have been able to compete with the charm Ronald Reagan brought to the Republican ticket, but Carter sure did change the future when he nominated RBG to the US Court of Appeals in 1980. Thank you, President Carter. While you may have lost the election that November, you certainly changed the future of my rights as a woman. But I clearly didn't know that at the time. When Reagan officially won the election in the midst of the Iran Hostage crisis and I watched my mom cry at the results, I penned an essay I've referred to often in my adulthood. In it, I wrote:

> *Hi I'm lisa. I want to know why there are wars. The hostages might be freed but, if we have more wars they'll take away more people. And Reagan, he is not doing anything about it. He is fighting against girls so they can't work. What about if you're poor. I just don't know why dumb Reagan won.*

I was spot on and fully entitled to my heartbreak. Little did I know that Carter planted the seeds of justice in that court appointment and that Justice Ginsburg had my back—and my future.

When we left the 70s in the rearview and I was squarely living out my tweens, my mom, brother, and I found ourselves on a once-in-a-lifetime trip to the Museum of Modern Art in New York City. Upon laying my naïve eyeballs on Yves Klein's Blue Monochrome, I predictably announced, "I could have done that. It's just a blue canvas."

My mom responded, "But you didn't."

Challenge accepted.

One problem: I never actually had the knack for art. I've always identified more with the cash register part of that pottery studio memory. Today, I see being a patron of art and being surrounded by art as a privilege. It's also part of my DNA. Grandma Sue picked up her paint brush for the first time in her 40s. She then became a well-recognized and award-winning naturalist, all while tending to *her* flock of sheep, four kids, various grandkids, and my grandfather, a verbose, gray-haired man who would have relished a long night of conversation over coffee and cigarettes, hashing out the merits of my justice jag.

Fast forward to 2018, when I buzzed over to 1508 U St. NW to see whether the building would work for an office expansion. I paused first to take note of its blank wall. That, I thought, would make a stellar backdrop for a mural. At that moment, the image of Justice Ginsburg releasing a flock of birds began to take shape in my mind, and two-and-a-half years later, hundreds of people would gather at the folds of her brick robes and say goodbye.

Our mural wouldn't cloak the wall without a fight. It took a long minute to negotiate and eventually close on the building. That's because the seller clearly wasn't confident I qualified, being a woman buyer. He openly questioned the company and our viability, and he shopped our offer for something better despite our nine strong years in business. He put off ratifying the contract, pushed back on the terms, and dragged his feet, telling me my SBA financing would, ironically at this point, take too much time. When we went under contract, he wouldn't allow me to inspect the property without an escort, and when we finally got to the closing table, three weeks late because of seller delays, he wouldn't give me keys to the building until the funds were in his bank account. Never mind I was then the legal owner. No problem. I just changed the locks. And the building is better off. So is the memory of Justice Ginsburg, who taught me that my right to own the building is protected. And I would persist.

So much of the credit for transforming the exterior of our building goes to the muralist, Rose Jaffe. Pre-Ginsburg, 1508 U Street was a mansion transformed into a little cubicle farm. In 2019, Rose offered the genius of mixed media to give Justice Ginsburg—small in stature, but larger than life—true visual magnitude. Her likeness on that wall eclipses the physical limitation of the brick. To visit her image there is to always look up, to be enveloped by her draped robes. The birds she is releasing invite us all to soar.

As I joined so many others at the mural at an impromptu vigil the weekend after Justice Ginsberg died, I did so promising her—and my mom and grandma Sue and my cousin Richard—to fight for a just tomorrow. I have them to thank for reminding me that breaking those barriers isn't just my right as a woman and as a member of the LGBTQ community, but it's my obligation. At Flock, we believe that being political in our pursuit of justice is our obligation, too. Today, it's even more of a calling, and I've become increasingly committed to amplifying my voice as a self-elected justice warrior and as a person in the business world. It's precisely why I've spent what seems like five years penning these chapters—and feeling no risk in the controversy or disagreement my words might inspire.

DON'T BE AFRAID OF CONTROVERSY

That racial justice is still considered by many in the US to be controversial is, honestly, a bit demoralizing. However, a cursory look at the headlines most days reinforces that this is true. It is not, however, an accurate proposition or a sustainable one.

It is long past time for the business community to quit thinking that their "diversity" and "inclusion" efforts are enough to address racism in our society. Such efforts not only put whiteness at the center of the conversation, but they also suggest that having a wide-ranging hue of faces on the employee roster does anything to address the entrenched and systematic racism that has existed for centuries in this country. It's time that businesses become actively, unreservedly anti-racist. As of this moment in history, it is no longer possible in the United States to plan for a thoughtful, purposeful, and successful business future without taking a path that is deliberately anti-racist, progressive, and built on the principles of equity and abundance.

In her well-received book, *The Sum of Us*, author Heather McGhee writes:

> "What we've got now just isn't working. When the rules of the game allow a small minority of participants to capture most of the gains, at a certain point (for example, when the entire middle class owns less than the wealthiest 1 percent of Americans), fewer people can start businesses, invest in their families, and invent new ideas and solutions—and then it isn't a problem just for those families. Ultimately, having millions of people with potential on the sidelines because they have too much debt and not enough opportunity saps the vitality of the entire economy. There's a

growing body of literature that shows that inequality itself impedes a country's economic growth—even more than the factors policy makers have emphasized in the past: liberalizing trade policies, controlling inflation, and reducing national debt. And America's racial inequality is not only the most extreme manifestation of our inequality, but also setting up the scaffolding of hierarchy that increasingly, few people of any race can climb." (272)

Let's think about that for a minute, then self-elect to become anti-racist individuals and companies. At Flock, we made this pledge:

- Our company will cultivate and sustain an inclusive, anti-racist workforce.
- We will no longer make excuses or exceptions for clients or residents who are racist toward our team.
- We will no longer look the other way when industry peers openly strategize workarounds for fair housing, vouchers, and operations in predominantly Black and brown neighborhoods.
- We will continually seek equity in senior management positions.
- We will advocate for programs that build bridges to better employment for Black, Indigenous, and other people of color.
- We will intensify our challenges to our industry and to its racist past. We will work toward rewriting a future that untangles toxic and predatory policies that have only served to benefit white property owners. We will begin

more formal efforts to challenge housing law and policy that is rooted in discrimination and inequity.

- We will not continue to lead quietly. We will leverage our large and growing community to act against racism. And we must.

Even a company with the best intentions is building wealth and success in a system that was built on stolen land with stolen labor. American capitalism has long supported white business owners, disenfranchised BIPOC potential business owners, justified and benefited from systemic racism, and promoted the benefits of whiteness as if race were a skill set rather than a question of the birds and the bees. It doesn't matter if these inequitable policies and practices predate us. When they were put into play doesn't mean that we don't benefit today. Because by design, we do—at least as white folks with privilege.

We've been deliberate about our anti-racism work at Flock. To date, it has included everything from assessing the values alignment of our vendors to creating a racial justice team to study our operations and policies to providing training on racism for our staff. In 2020, when we first closed to honor Juneteenth, we made it clear to our clients and residents that the closure wasn't just a political gesture but also a personal one. Each of our Black team members (and other team members of color) have experienced explicit and implicit racism while working for Roost DC, Nest DC, and Starling DC. They have been denied access to units, been recorded while working, had police called when they entered buildings, and been asked to leave when on-site. This behavior is unacceptable, but sadly not uncommon. We also made sure our clients, residents, friends, and fans knew that Flocksters would have the holiday to reflect, restore their energy, or resist, but the building would remain open. That's because we were in the midst of that summer's uprisings and wanted to make our space available to protestors needing water, snacks, restrooms, pumping stations, or power stations.

We also let our stakeholders know that we were actively analyzing our procurement policies to ensure they were aligned with our values and mission. Local procurement from diverse vendors has always been a top priority for Flock. Nevertheless, there are still times when we can't buy locally to meet the needs of the project. We consequently began evaluating our broader procurement efforts, which resulted in our decision to significantly reduce and, ultimately, discontinue our spending with Home Depot. The company founder, who still generates wealth from the company's stock, had publicly announced his support of the Trump re-election campaign.[58] Lowes, in contrast, expressed their support for Black Lives Matter and initiated other programs to support small businesses.[59] We absolutely know both companies have problematic practices and track records, and our continued analysis will guide our future procurement practices. We expect this work to be iterative and based on research and real-time

[58]Ciment, "People Are Calling to Boycott Home Depot after Its Co-Founder Said He Was Voting for Trump and Encouraged Others to Do the Same."

[59]Repko, "'Talk Less and Do More': Lowe's CEO Marvin Ellison Says Corporate Leaders Must Step up Diversity Efforts."

information. We also hope that others will follow our lead and encourage our vendors to consider their own sourcing decisions and impact. Many have done so, in a heartening testament to how our values are aligned.

REIMAGINING CAPITALISM: JUST CAPITALISM

In the property management house we custom built, we are living comfortably on the outskirts of town and are aiming to build a whole new business utopia. We are bold in challenging traditional notions of how capitalism might inform the trajectory of our company. I've been able to operate as a vocal advocate for a new model of just capitalism that leans into an abundance model, versus unjust capitalism, which is grounded in scarcity. That very approach is a challenge to capitalism as we know it. It is also, I believe, the best path forward for humanity. Conveniently, for someone like me who is dedicated to maintaining financial stability, just capitalism does not have to be at the expense of profitability and success. I'm arguing that you *can* have it all. You just have to solve for what "all" really means. For me, all means much more than cold, hard cash, and it is as concerned with the stakeholder as it is with the shareholder.

I intentionally structured my flock of companies to avoid the obligations inherent in catering only to the shareholder, who, by design, is invested in financial profits. A stakeholder, in contrast, can include individuals, governments, industries, the environment, and more. Much has been written about the shareholder paradigm in business—and there have been contemporary and increasingly vocal invitations to shift the conversation and business practice to one that considers stakeholders. The heart of capitalism has been rooted in profitability as if it's manifest destiny. When we measure profitability in terms of impact on stakeholders and shareholders, the value proposition accelerates. There can be a hybrid model—just capitalism—wherein we seek profits and have a positive net impact on the social, political, and environmental ecosystems. Simply put, as Rebecca Henderson explains so well in her book "Reimagining Capitalism in a World on Fire": "The only way we will solve the problems that we face is if we can find a way to balance the power of the market with the power of inclusive institutions, and purpose-driven businesses committed to the health of the society could play an important role in making this happen."[60]

In its purest form, capitalism is a system that serves the private sector in its quest to make a profit. Presumably, that profit is monetary. In a just world (yet to be realized), the wealth generated by capitalism would find its way to the whole of society and create opportunities that give us all a pathway to prosperity. In our current model, it creates a society of haves and have-nots. As Heather McGhee further notes in "The Sum of Us": "wealth is where your financial freedom is determined by compounding interest on decisions made long before you were born. That is why the Black-white wealth gap is growing despite gains in Black education and earnings,

---

[60]Henderson, *Reimagining Capitalism in a World on Fire*.

and why the typical Black household only owns $17,600 in assets."[61]

Capitalism assumes there is an equally accessible entry point, that pulling yourself up by the bootstraps is an opportunity afforded to all. We know this isn't the case. Where you were born and to whom will be a predictor of your agency. Layer on education, gender, race, and zip code, and the deck can either be heavily stacked for or against you. And while capitalism is proclaimed to be the "great equalizer," it relies heavily on *inequality* to work. Capitalism requires a low-wage segment of people who have adapted to living with less, so others can enjoy much more. The average American isn't able to weather a $400 emergency. We need a more just model. We need an alternative to traditional capitalism. What we have now leaves too many behind to suffer the crushing devastation of natural disasters, pandemics, economic shifts, climate change, racism, and so much more. That shouldn't be okay. No matter the industry. No matter your politics.

Justice-driven business owners ask: *Does traditional capitalism offer authentic opportunity? Does traditional capitalism function as an equalizer? Does traditional capitalism make us all free or just maintain the freedom of the already free?* I believe that—and behave as if—the answers to those questions above are a resounding no. Because, obviously, capitalism is failing too many of us. Still, I'm not inclined to toss the entirety of capitalist principles out the window. There are, in fact, some appealing advantages delivered by capitalism and a free and

---

[61] McGhee, The Sum of Us, 277.

fair market, and innovation is at the very top of that list, along with consumer choice, but unless capitalism is reimagined, we'll continue to suffer the inequality it perpetuates because profit-first capitalist paradigms have left too little room for justice. When we introduce justice into modern capitalism (or just capitalism as I've been calling it), we can entertain and implement policies and practices that create more level playing fields. Those investments can help us leapfrog the zero-sum game we're all victims of.

Rebecca Henderson, renowned economist and author of "Rethinking Capitalism in a World On Fire," says this about paths to equity: "Rebuilding our institutions requires the development of new ways of behaving and new ways of believing... We will not reimagine capitalism unless we rediscover the values on which capitalism has always been based, and have the courage and the skill to integrate them into the day-to-day fabric of business. To pretend that this is not the case is to critically misrepresent the truth of our current situation. We are destroying the world and the social fabric in service of a quick buck, and we need to move beyond the simple maximization of shareholder value before we bring the whole system crashing down around our heads."[62] Henderson reminds us that the courage to live our values will play a critical role in driving necessary changes. I've self-elected to lean into my courage by creating a justice-driven business that can benefit from the best parts of capitalism while leaving the singular focus on cash profits behind.

---

[62] Henderson, *Reimagining Capitalism in a World on Fire*, 44.

Nationally and globally, we should be laser-focused on sorting out the good from the bad, and we should do it quickly. Most people have been unable to enjoy those benefits, especially as massive businesses and monopolies have dominated the marketplace. Inequity is itself a currency among traditional capitalists. It's a broken system for those it doesn't serve well, and an increasing number among us are falling into that category.

FALSE STARTS—THE SHRINKING NUMBER OF STARTUPS

If capitalism were working, new startups would not be steadily declining. Fundamentally, we need them for a sustainable and robust economy. Steve Blank makes a powerful point when discussing the merits of a lean startup model:

> Using lean methods across a portfolio of startups will result in fewer failures than using traditional methods. A lower startup failure rate could have profound economic consequences. Today the forces of disruption, globalization, and regulation are buffeting the economies of every country. Established industries are rapidly shedding jobs, many of which will never return. Employment growth in the 21st century will have to come from new ventures, so we all have a vested interest in fostering an environment that helps them succeed, grow, and hire more workers. The creation of an innovation economy that's driven by

the rapid expansion of startups has never been more imperative.[63]

Mr. Blank is not alone in his thinking. As Leigh Buchanan noted in *Inc.* Magazine:

The Kauffman Foundation, citing its own research and drawing on U.S. Census data, concluded that the number of companies less than a year old had declined as a share of all businesses by nearly 44 percent between 1978 and 2012. And those declines swept across industries, including tech. Meanwhile, the Brookings Institution, also using Census data, established that the number of new businesses is down across the country and that more businesses are dying than are being born. All this at a time when entrepreneurship had reached its cultural apex and was widely viewed as the sole sizzling ember in an otherwise cooling economy. The business and academic worlds were left slack-jawed: How could this be? The implications are huge. "New businesses are disproportionately responsible for the innovation that drives productivity and economic growth, and they account for virtually all net new job creation," says John Dearie, executive vice president for policy at the Financial Services Forum. "I would say, as a policy person, this is nothing short of a national emergency."[64]

---

[63] Blank, "Why the Lean Startup Changes Everything."
[64] Buchanan, "American Entrepreneurship Is Actually Vanishing. Here's Why."

I'm glad to know I've got sizzle as an entrepreneur, but I would like to be in good company. When our economy depends on small businesses for a hefty percent of job creation, what happens when the little fish are just a behemoth buffet? In 2021, the Congressional Research Service reported that 46.8% of the workforce is employed by small businesses.[65] The inevitable outcomes are: low wages, accelerated inequalities and wealth gaps, underemployment, and uninsured or underinsured gig workers who can't afford healthcare and for whom the middle class is simply a dream. Without small, purpose- and justice-driven companies emerging and meeting demands for high quality jobs, Americans lose purchase and purchasing power. Alissa Quart, in her powerful book "Squeezed," tells the devastating story of a declining middle class that disproportionately impacts women, mothers, and, most of all, women of color with children.[66] The costs of education now often outpace the benefit of the degree in the marketplace. Add a child (or two), and the opportunity costs of parenthood are often insurmountable, leaving those who might like to follow in their parents' footsteps many steps behind them. Desperate to get ahead and with increasingly limited professional opportunities, they are ill prepared to deal with an increasingly high cost of living.

The decline of unions has lined up with these trends, so that now more than ever, employees are left to fend for themselves in states that neither mandate living wages,

---

[65] Dilger, "Small Business Administration and job creation."
[66] Quart, *Squeezed: Why Our Families Can't Afford America.*

pre-school, or childcare access, nor hold the employer responsible for paid time off for illness or rest. This dynamic favors almost exclusively the needs of the shareholder at the expense of the stakeholder. John Booth, in his thrilling and frightening book, "The Price of Tomorrow," contrasts pre-technology economies with our now nearly global reliance on technology. He argues this will inevitably lead to our demise unless we take action soon. Booth's recommendation is that we bet on deflation as our pathway out of harm's way and initiate a redistribution of wealth and resources (like universal basic income) to avoid the train wreck we're otherwise speeding toward.[67] Booth's thinking is co-signed by Rebecca Henderson who states simply: "Building a just and sustainable society, requires not only the protection of property rights and political rights but also civil rights, or equality before the law. No society can be inclusive if it discriminates between groups in the provision of public goods such as justice, security, education, and health."[68] I'm going to say it again, louder for those who haven't been paying attention: **justice is a public good**, not a reserved right for a few.

Perhaps traditional capitalism is simply outdated. Maybe we can no longer shield ourselves from its toxic underpinnings and reliance on disparity. The information revolution, the emergence of technology, and the internet age have reduced true opportunity for those with fewer resources and

---

[67] Booth, *The Price of Tomorrow: Why Deflation Is the Key to an Abundant Future*.

[68] Henderson, *Reimagining Capitalism in a World on Fire*, 216.

who were unable or chose not to pursue education beyond high school. Low-wage, low-skilled jobs are more abundant while technical jobs offering entry to the middle class have faded. A rich article by Dani Alexis Ryskam published in *The Atlantic* examines the fictional life of The Simpsons, in which two and a half children can be tended to by a stay-at-home parent while the other enjoys the wages and benefits of a union job and heads home in the family car for dinner at six.[69] That lifestyle may have been accessible in the 90s, during the show's earliest years, but it is pure fiction today.

Am I arguing that we need a total redistribution of wealth? Not necessarily. But I do propose something more just, something human that would be transformational for so many. That means dignified housing for all and access to high-quality education and healthcare. If everyone had these three needs covered, even to the most basic extent, the emotionally taxing energy of trying to make ends meet would be relieved. People could focus on the opportunity that capitalism may offer and escape the borderline or functional poverty or paycheck-to-paycheck lifestyle most are living.

Just capitalism requires businesses to factor in, well, justice. It invites alternative key performance indicators, like empathy, stewardship, abundance, and servant leadership. When these principles are applied, the magnitude of the win is hard to ignore. My fervent hope is that those of you reading, who would like to become entrepreneurs or who want to recreate the business you have to make it more just and

---

[69] Ryskamp, "The Life in 'The Simpsons' Is No Longer Attainable."

values-driven, will apply the principles of a lean startup, servant leadership, and differentiation to stand out and stand up for justice. If you do, I believe that the company will not only reap profits for you, but will also make your entire community stronger, from your staff members to your fanbase.

I encourage you to anchor yourself in your purpose and values. As you saw from Flock's values at the beginning of this book, your core values don't have to be complicated. They just have to be consistent, and they must be woven through everything you do. Our service-based business could not be best-in-class without our undying commitment to empathy. Choose values that are core to what you do and what you believe in.

Self-elect to differentiate your brand. Making this decision when you're a justice-driven business not only helps you gain market share, but it also allows you to build a fan club that shares your commitment to leaving your community and your world better than you found them.

Employ a servant-leadership model because giving your team the support and space to do their work makes their jobs more valuable. Sharing what you can, from profits to ownership to leadership, builds team cohesion and buy-in. Operate as a perpetual startup, recognizing that innovation is an engine that can propel your team forward to amazing distances. When there's always something next, your workplace can be one of excitement and one where people are excited to show up for the job.

Optimize operations by regularly assessing what systems and tools are working and which need to be released to the wild. Trust your team to lead and to make changes when change is needed. Your business will be more efficient, and your team will be more satisfied.

Finally, cultivate a culture that brings everyone together. You can do this through creating a casual atmosphere and building community, as we did before we could afford envy-inspiring benefits. Importantly, being anchored in justice does some of the work of creating a culture that makes your colleagues feel like family. When you're not afraid to take a stand for racial justice, when you focus on a broad group of stakeholders instead of a narrow group of shareholders, when you embrace abundance and eschew scarcity, your culture can't be anything but strong. When you self-elect to do good financially by doing good socially, everyone wins. If that's not the best way of looking at profit, I don't know what is.

EPILOGUE: TAKE CARE OF ONE ANOTHER

I f ever there was an industry worth transforming, it would be elder care. And it's precisely where this book began. I offered elder care, whether I knew it or not, to my bestie Myrtle. I self-elected, even as a young girl, to care for those whose lifelines weren't accessible and whose family was too far away or not there at all. This became a tradition for me over time, and like most of my passions, it found its way into my work.

In college, together with Frances, I spent many afternoons and weekends with Evelyn Sabra Hoke working a modestly paid job as her lady reader. In pre-internet days, Frances and I would scour the campus job board for any opportunity to earn cash. Folks from around the community would handwrite notes and pin them on the corkboard, waiting for a match. Frances plucked Miss Hoke's index card, penned beautifully, requesting afternoon and weekend lady readers for company and household tasks. It was the perfect match for the three of us.

Miss Hoke was 93, blind, and homebound. She started every call with this information, following it up with, "...and I appreciate shopping by telephone!" I dialed the phone for her quite often. With her lady readers, she maintained a window to the world. There were a handful of us passing through, all of us busy college girls trying to make the ends of college needs meet. Miss Hoke was a fairly straightforward charge. We made simple meals or ran out for her favorite fast food. We pulled old, yellowed newspapers from "wall street," the hallway packed floor to ceiling with a decade of the *Arizona Daily Star*. She slept stretched out on a davenport using a stack of newspaper, frosted with a pillow as an ottoman.

Miss Hoke lived in a tin can of a trailer home, what I called her aluminum attic. As I shimmied around her space, I was aware it was exploding with everything from vintage cameras to 15 years of phone books. Hoarding wasn't as much in the lexicon then, but it describes her lifestyle well. My first day as a lady reader was more lady sleuth: I was charged with finding her teeth, which had made their way into her old lady garbage.

Every task I performed for Miss Hoke was a treasured moment. We sorted the photos she took during her two-tour Peace Corps stint in her 70s after leaving the faculty of Ball State University. She described settling in Swaziland, camera in hand, charged with "documenting history through photography." When her storytelling paused, she asked us to chant with her while she did her maraca exercises. She rattled her instruments, side to side, slowly but with passion. "War on war!" she huffed. "War on war!!!" she puffed. We were with her all the way.

Soon we started spending time with Miss Hoke as a three-some because we enjoyed being together that much. Frances and I exchanged glances as she told us stories of her friend, Ethel Heimlich, who slept on the sofa to save expenses while they both worked at BSU. Later Miss Hoke would offer, "I've never been with a man!" adding, "Or a woman... not really."

No matter what we did, I was at home with Miss Hoke. Home is where we're taken care of, safe, and secure. She would send us off after our shifts with a wave and a scratchy, drawn-out demand: "Take care of one another. Just take care of one another." Once again, challenge accepted. As long as homes need a caregiver and the world needs fighters for justice, our Flock will be flying high, and so will I.

Note: In late March of 2020, I looked around the "Zoom," and I said to our team, "Don't look back on this unique moment and time and regret how you chose to spend it." I was talking to myself as much as I was to them. And with that, live in justice and enjoy this book at least half as much as I enjoyed writing it.

SPEAKING & CONSULTING

Lisa is available for fireside chats (a favorite), as well as panels and presentations of all sizes. She's also up for a good 1:1 chat! You can reach her at lisa@meetlisawise.com and she'll look forward to connecting.

ABOUT FLOCK,
birdSEED, BirdWatch

Flock DC is a family of real estate management companies that tend to over 2 billion dollars in property. *www.flock-dc.com*

BirdWatch is a people-first, technology-driven national company that delivers maintenance and improvement services for homeowners. *www.birdwatch.com*

birdSEED is a housing justice foundation that gives BIPOC first-time homebuyers no-strings down payment grants. birdSEED is operated and funded by Flock DC and BirdWatch. *www.birdseed.org*

10% of the proceeds from this book will be donated to The birdSEED Foundation. *www.birdseed.org*

ABOUT THE AUTHOR

Growing up throughout rural Idaho, lisa was surrounded by love, though short on resources and stability. She sought security by building businesses from a young age, starting with her first of many enterprises, The Sherlock Holmes Detective Agency. Offices were open for business in her parents' backyard tool shed, but clients and their mysteries never materialized. Like any passionate entrepreneur, she moved on, unphased, to the next hustle.

Today, lisa successfully oversees real estate management and technology enterprises anchored in justice and profitable by design. In 2020, she founded and launched birdSEED, a housing justice initiative granting no-strings down payment grants to first time BIPOC buyers. In 2022, birdSEED was named a world-changing idea by *Fast Company*. You will hear lisa declare often: "I want to get rich and give it away!!!" She lives in Washington, DC with her little family.

Social Media Handles

LinkedIn: *@lisawise*
Facebook: */lisa.wise*
Instagram: */wiselis*
self-elected.com

BIBLIOGRAPHY

"1% For the Planet—Homepage." *1% For the Planet—Homepage*, https://www.onepercentfortheplanet.org/.

"2021 Talent Attraction and Retention Survey." *Willis Towers Watson*, 16 Sept. 2021, https://www.wtwco.com/en-US/Insights/2021/09/2021-talent-attraction-and-retention-survey.

"About the Stakeholder Theory." *Stakeholder Theory*, http://stakeholdertheory.org/about/.

Baldridge, Rebecca. "What Is a Startup?" *Forbes*, Forbes Magazine, 4 Feb. 2022, https://www.forbes.com/advisor/investing/what-is-a-startup/.

Balova, Anastacia. "Should 10-Year-Old Companies Call Themselves Startups." *LinkedIn*, LinkedIn, 18 Aug. 2021, https://www.linkedin.com/pulse/startup-definition-why-10-year-old-companies-call-startups-balova/.

"Barbara Kruger—Your Body Is a Battleground." *Public Delivery*, 12 Oct. 2021, https://publicdelivery.org/barbara-kruger-battleground/.

Baskin, Morgan. "DCHA Says Thousands of Units Are Nearly Uninhabitable. Tenants Want to Know: What's Next?" *Washington City Paper*, 14 Feb. 2019.

Blank, Steve. "Why the Lean Start-up Changes Everything." *Harvard Business Review*, May 2013, https://hbr.org/2013/05/why-the-lean-start-up-changes-everything.

Booth, Jeff. *The Price of Tomorrow: Why Deflation Is the Key to an Abundant Future*. Stanley Press, 2020.

Bower, Joseph L, and Lynn S Paine. "The Error at the Heart of Corporate Leadership." *Harvard Business Review*, 14 July 2021, https://hbr.org/2017/05/the-error-at-the-heart-of-corporate-leadership.

Brooks, Arthur C. "The Secret to Happiness at Work." *The Atlantic*, Atlantic Media Company, 7 Apr. 2022, https://www.theatlantic.com/family/archive/2021/09/dream-job-values-happiness/619951/.

Buchanan, Leigh. "American Entrepreneurship Is Actually Vanishing. Here's Why." *Inc.com*, Inc., 1 Apr. 2015, https://www.inc.com/magazine/201505/leigh-buchanan/the-vanishing-startups-in-decline.html.

Calarco, Jessica McCrory. "Why Rich Kids Are so Good at the Marshmallow Test." *The Atlantic*, Atlantic Media Company, 28 Apr. 2021, https://www.theatlantic.com/family/archive/2018/06/marshmallow-test/561779/.

"CareerBuilder Survey Reveals a More Flexible Future Workforce." *Press Room | Career Builder*, 15 Dec. 2020, https://press.careerbuilder.com/2020-12-15-CareerBuilder-Survey-Reveals-a-More-Flexible-Future-Workforce.

Ciment, Shoshy. "People Are Calling to Boycott Home Depot after Its Co-Founder Said He Was Voting for Trump and Encouraged Others to Do the Same." *Business Insider*, Business Insider, 1 Nov. 2020, https://www.businessinsider.com/shoppers-boycott-home-depot-after-founder-says-will-vote-trump-2020-11.

Clear, James. "40 Years of Stanford Research Found That People with This One Quality Are More Likely to Succeed." *James Clear*, 4 Feb. 2020, https://jamesclear.com/delayed-gratification.

Corbett, Holly. "How Companies Are Helping to Close the Racial Wealth Gap." *Forbes*, Forbes Magazine, 27 Apr. 2021, https://www.forbes.com/sites/hollycorbett/2021/04/27/how-companies-are-helping-to-close-the-racial-wealth-gap/?sh=cdd61822bbb3.

Decker, Vivienne. "Farmgirl Flowers: A Blooming Startup That Is Disrupting the Flower Industry." *Forbes*, Forbes Magazine, 22 Dec. 2015, https://www.forbes.com/sites/viviennedecker/2015/12/22/farmgirl-flowers-a-blooming-startup-thats-disrupting-the-flower-industry/?sh=71afe9a76385.

Denning, Steve. "Making Sense of Shareholder Value: 'the World's Dumbest Idea'." *Forbes*, Forbes Magazine, 10 Dec. 2021, https://www.forbes.com/sites/stevedenning/2017/07/17/making-sense-of-shareholder-value-the-worlds-dumbest-idea/?sh=457d9fc02a7e.

Desmond, Matthew. *Evicted: Poverty and Profit in the American City.* Broadway Books, 2017.

Dilger, Robert Jay. *Small Business Administration and Job Creation.* https://sgp.fas.org/crs/misc/R41523.pdf.

Duhigg, Charles. *The Power of Habit*. Penguin Random House, 2014.

"Employee Retention in Property Management." *Home365*, Home365 | Property Management Reinvented, 9 Dec. 2021, https://www.home365.co/employee-retention-in-property-management/.

Entrepreneurs' Organization. "The Proven Methodology for Running a Successful Business Sustainably and Prosperously with the Greater Good at Heart." *Inc.com*, Inc., 13 Oct. 2020, https://www.inc.com/entrepreneurs-organization/how-to-run-a-successful-business-while-simultaneously-elevating-humanity.html.

Friedman, Jared. "How to Get Startup Ideas: Startup Ideas, Problems to Solve, Becoming a Founder: Y Combinator." *YC Startup Library*, 2020, https://www.ycombinator.com/library/8g-how-to-get-startup-ideas.

Friedman, Milton. "A Friedman Doctrine—the Social Responsibility of Business Is to Increase Its Profits." *The New York Times*, The New York Times, 13 Sept. 1970, https://www.nytimes.com/1970/09/13/archives/a-friedman-doctrine-the-social-responsibility-of-business-is-to.html.

Heath, Thomas. "Perspective | Managing Real Estate, Building Wealth." *The Washington Post*, WP Company, 21 Dec. 2019, https://www.washingtonpost.com/business/economy/managing-real-estate-building-wealth/2019/12/18/df01ff9e-1dd1-11ea-8d58-5ac3600967a1_story.html.

Henderson, Rebecca. *Reimagining Capitalism in a World on Fire*. PublicAffairs, 2020.

"Here's What Your Turnover and Retention Rates Should Look Like." 22 Mar. 2021, https://www.glassdoor.com/employers/blog/turnover-retention-rates/.

Holtzman, Ben. "The Age of Predatory Inclusion." *Shelterforce*, 11 June 2020, https://shelterforce.org/2020/06/11/the_age_of_predatory_inclusion/.

Jenkins, Ryan. "Statistics Exposing What Generation Z Wants from the Workplace." *Ryan Jenkins Next Generation Catalyst, Speaker & Blogger*, https://blog.ryan-jenkins.com/statistics-exposing-what-generation-z-wants-from-the-workplace.

Kahlenberg, Richard D. "Why Did It Take So Long for Class-Based School Integration to Take Hold?" *The Atlantic*, Atlantic Media Company, 2 July 2016, https://www.theatlantic.com/education/archive/2016/07/why-did-it-take-so-long-for-class-based-school-integration-to-take-hold/489863/.

Keyes, Ralph. "Ask Not Where This Quote Came From." *The Washington Post*, 4 June 2006, https://www.washingtonpost.com/archive/opinions/2006/06/04/ask-not-where-this-quote-came-from/ca3a139f-0060-477e-9693-48b08f6d0e20/.

Kuchler, Cheryl Beth. "The Power of People and Leaving a Legacy (by Jeff Hoffman)." *CEO Think Tank*, 28 Feb. 2021, https://ceothinktank.com/thinking-tank/the-power-of-people-and-leaving-a-legacy-by-jeff-hoffman.

Lerner, Michele. "Report: Median Sales Price of Houses in D.C. Now Exceeds $1 Million." *The Washington Post*, WP Company, 18 Nov. 2020, https://www.washingtonpost.com/business/2020/12/02/report-median-sales-price-houses-dc-now-exceeds-1-million/.

Lloyd, Alcynna. "Decade in Review: Number of U.S. Renters Surpasses 100 Million." *HousingWire*, 12 Mar. 2020, https://www.housingwire.com/articles/decade-in-review-number-of-u-s-renters-surpasses-100-million/.

McGhee, Heather C. *The Sum of Us: What Racism Costs Everyone and How We Can Prosper Together*. One World, 2021.

McGrady, Vanessa. "New Survey: Three Main Reasons Why Millennials Quit Their Jobs." *Forbes*, Forbes Magazine, 29 Nov. 2016, https://www.forbes.com/sites/vanessamcgrady/2016/11/29/survey-three-main-reasons-why-millennials-quit-their-jobs/?sh=72eb6dad22ae.

Mehta, Seema. "Mixing Politics and Parsley: Why This Spice Seller Spent $700,000-plus on Facebook Ads for Trump's Impeachment." *Los Angeles Times*, Los Angeles Times, 7 Dec. 2019, https://www.latimes.com/politics/story/2019-12-07/penzeys-spices-spending-big-on-facebook-ads-supporting-trump-impeachment.

Novak, Michael. *Business as a Calling*. Free Press, 1996.

Organization, Entrepreneurs'. "The Proven Methodology for Running a Successful Business Sustainably and Prosperously with the Greater Good at Heart." *Inc.com*, Inc., 13 Oct. 2020, https://www.inc.com/

entrepreneurs-organization/how-to-run-a-successful-business-while-simultaneously-elevating-humanity.html.

"Patrick O. Brown." *Wikipedia*, Wikimedia Foundation, 22 Apr. 2022, https://en.wikipedia.org/wiki/Patrick_O._Brown.

"Profit." *Merriam-Webster*, https://www.merriam-webster.com/dictionary/profit.

Quart, Alissa. *Squeezed: Why Our Families Can't Afford America*. HarperCollins Publishers, 2018.

Ravari, Ali, et al. "Work Values and Job Satisfaction." *Nursing Ethics*, vol. 20, no. 4, 2012, pp. 448–458., https://doi.org/10.1177/0969733012458606.

Ren, Ting. "Value Congruence as a Source of Intrinsic Motivation." *Kyklos*, vol. 63, no. 1, 2010, pp. 94–109., https://doi.org/10.1111/j.1467-6435.2010.00462.x.

Reneau, Annie. "Penzey's Spices Is 'Looting' Its Own Kenosha Store in a Statement about Priorities." *Upworthy*, Upworthy, 31 Aug. 2020, https://www.upworthy.com/penzeys-spices-looting-its-own-store-for-racial-justice.

Repko, Melissa. "'Talk Less and Do More': Lowe's CEO Marvin Ellison Says Corporate Leaders Must Step up Diversity Efforts." *CNBC*, CNBC, 15 July 2020, https://www.cnbc.com/2020/07/01/lowes-ceo-marvin-ellison-says-corporate-leaders-must-step-up-diversity-efforts.html.

Ries, Eric. *The Lean Startup: How Today's Entrepreneurs Use Continuous Innovation to Create Radically Successful Businesses*. Crown Business, 2011.

Rosner, Helen, and Jonathan Kauffman. "The C.E.O. Who Called Trump a Racist (and Sold a Lot of

Spice Mix).” *The New Yorker*, 1 Feb. 2018, https://www.newyorker.com/culture/annals-of-gastronomy/ceo-who-called-trump-racist-penzeys-spice-mix.

Ryskamp, Dani Alexis. “The Life in ‘The Simpsons’ Is No Longer Attainable.” *The Atlantic*, Atlantic Media Company, 8 Feb. 2021, https://www.theatlantic.com/ideas/archive/2020/12/life-simpsons-no-longer-attainable/617499/.

Scott, Kim Malone. *Radical Candor: Be a Kick-Ass Boss without Losing Your Humanity*. St. Martin’s Press, 2019.

Semuels, Alana. “When Wall Street Is Your Landlord.” *The Atlantic*, Atlantic Media Company, 8 Apr. 2019, https://www.theatlantic.com/technology/archive/2019/02/single-family-landlords-wall-street/582394/.

“US Workers Willing to Compromise on Salary for the Right Benefits, Company Culture, and Career Growth Opportunities.” *Go to Hays USA*, 16 Oct. 2017, https://www.hays.com/press-release-do-not-use-/content/us-workers-willing-to-compromise-on-salary-for-the-right-benefits-company-culture-and-career-growth-opportunities.

Wise, lisa. “Opinion | Housing Justice Is a Basic Human Right.” *The Washington Post*, WP Company, 16 Jan. 2021, https://www.washingtonpost.com/opinions/local-opinions/housing-justice-is-a-basic-human-right/2021/01/07/74e6db4c-4086-11eb-8db8-395dedaaa036_story.html.

Zak, Paul J. “The Neuroscience of Trust, Management Behaviors That Foster Employee Engagement.” *Harvard Business Review*, 31 Aug. 2021, https://hbr.org/2017/01/the-neuroscience-of-trust.